Crisis management in small US businesses.

Georgia R. Maldonado

Abstract

As a critical infrastructure, the US electricity grid supplies electricity to 340 million

people within eight separate regions. The power infrastructure is vulnerable to many

types of disasters capable of severing supplies of electricity. The impact on the

employees and communities when small- and medium-size enterprises are shut down due

to disasters can be severe. The purpose of the quantitative comparative study was to

explore small- and medium-size enterprises crisis management strategies in the case of

power infrastructure vulnerabilities. Perceptions of small business leaders were probed

about crisis management planning relevant to three secondary factors: prior experience of

crises, threat perceptions, and planning self-efficacy. Participants completed an adapted

questionnaire instrument based on a five-point Likert scale for six sub-factors including

resilience through planning, financial impact, operational crisis management, the perfect

storm, the aftermath of survival, and atrophy. The instrument also measured three

additional factors to include, prior experience of crises, threat perceptions, and planning

self-efficacy, across seven types of crises. The results of this study indicated that of the

276 respondents, 104 had no crisis plans, but 172 did have crisis plans. Of those who had

implemented crisis plans, 19% had specific provisions to address power outages or

attacks on the electrical grid. Of the respondents who had not planned for power outages

nor experienced significant losses of power, a statistically significant number

acknowledged an external threat to their business. The majority of respondents indicated

that long-term planning was related to resilience; however, the migration of crisis

understanding into the planning process or implementation was not implemented. This

heightened awareness of potential crises without the corresponding development and implementation of mitigation crisis plans requires additional research to understand

drivers effecting the decision making process with crisis managers.

Table of Contents

List of Tables

List of Figures

Chapter 1: Introduction

A loss of critical power to sources of community stability such as small businesses interrupts quality of life and can also cause serious economic implications if power is not quickly restored (Farrell, Lave, & Granger, 2002; Kharchenko & Brezhnev, 2012; Mitroff & Alpaslan, 2003b). Businesses that are prepared for, or prone to, crises become a critical component of national crisis/disaster resiliency (Herbane, 2013), and for those businesses that maintain a level of preparedness, stand ready to react to disasters through predetermined plans and training (Haddow, Bullock, & Coppola, 2011). The present study was concentrated on how small businesses addressed crisis management as influenced by interruption of electrical power. Businesses rely on a stable electrical electricity grid and a brief or extended power outage can challenge the adequacies of crisis management plans.

Small businesses operate with the expectation that a regular supply of energy will be available and the need for redundant energy supplies is costly and unneeded. These expectations may not be based on historic, current, or future events of the US electricity grid. When planning for crises, consideration should be given to the current state of critical infrastructure that is essential for continuity of business. Businesses that fail to adequately assess vital continuity of business services and plan for their loss or interruption may prolong recovery time, experience financial and asset losses, and have a dramatic impact on employees and the community.

The US electricity grid is a critical infrastructure of interconnected electrical systems that produce usable energy and deliver the energy to consumers through a web of delivery components (Department of Energy, 2014; Grose, 2011; Koch & Kolasa, 2011; Petina, Murphy, & Gross, 2011). The power infrastructure is instrumental in maintaining not only the safety and security of the nation, but also fosters stability of the national socioeconomic environment and an uninterrupted quality of life (Farrell et al., 2002; Kharchenko & Brezhnev, 2012). Systems that are essential to the continuity of life must maintain an adequate level of resiliency when challenged by natural and manmade hazards (Department of Energy, 2013; Energy Information Administration, 2013). As a critical infrastructure, the US electricity grid supplies electricity to 340 million people within eight separate regions. North American Electric Reliability Corporation (NERC) regulates each of the eight regions (Figure 1) located in a large portion of North America to include the US, Canada, and a portion of Mexico (Energy Information Administration, 2013). Power production and distribution occurs through a system of nearly 7,000 power plants, over 19,000 generators, 20,000 large power transformers, and is supported with 540,000 miles of transmission lines (Department of Energy, 2014; Energy Information Administration, 2013). The inability of a single component within this system to be resilient when faced with hazards can cause a cascade of power failures across the nation affecting millions of people (American Society of Civil Engineers, 2014). While there is no guarantee against electricity grid failures, especially given the current state of the infrastructure components, preparation for outages can mitigate the impact

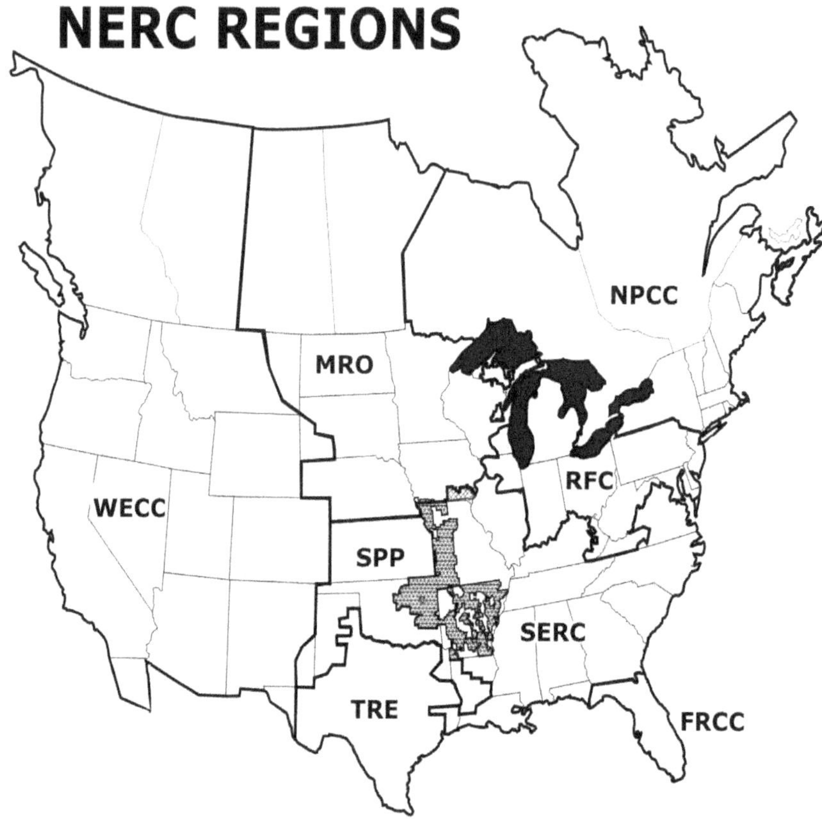

Figure 1. NERC Regions (Energy Information Administration, 2013).

on businesses and communities, they support. Communities also have an integral

role in supporting their imbedded businesses through identification and mitigation

of potential hazards including those associated with power supplies (Adams,

2008). However, businesses must be aware that while their communities should

be able to provide support during emergencies, local preparedness response

systems have limitations in resources and availabilities due to prioritization of

crises and budget shortfalls (Shughart, 2011).

Background

Mounting evidence supports the argument that the US electricity grid is vulnerable to disruption or destruction over large areas of the nation (Gaffney, 2014; Hancock, 2012; Thatcher, Brock, & Pendleton, 2013; Tretkof, 2010). The categories of risk to this critical infrastructure generally fit within the framework of either natural or human-caused disasters. Examples include coordinated cyber, physical, and blended terrorist (domestic or foreign) attacks, high-altitude detonation of a nuclear weapon, and major natural disasters such as earthquakes, tsunamis, hurricanes, pandemics (loss of staff critical to operations). Some recently identified risks to the electricity grid involve geomagnetic disturbances caused by solar storms. These particular risks are continuously assessed relative to their impact to societies and potential frequency of occurrence. The North American Electric Reliability Corporation and the U.S. Department of Energy described this class of geomagnetic disturbance as high-impact, low-frequency events that "have the potential to cause catastrophic impacts on the electric power system, but either rarely occur, or, in some cases, have never occurred" (North American Electric Reliability Corporation, 2010, p. 8). However, these natural or human-caused disasters do not encompass all of the risks associated with an electric infrastructure plagued by aging technologies and electricity grid components (Bakken, 2001; Faiers, Cook, & Neame, 2007; McKerchar & Evans, 2009). In addition to assessing the associated risks to the power supply, consideration has to be given to the impact on the end users. When considering the significance of the disruption of electric power, Chang, Mcdaniels, Mikawoz, and Peterson, (2007) referenced the direct impact on society as well as the "triggering or exacerbating disruptions to water, transportation, and other systems, which in turn cause further societal impacts" (p. 275). Chang et al. termed these close and overlapping connections as "infrastructure failure interdependencies (IFIs)" (p. 276) as shown in Figure 2.

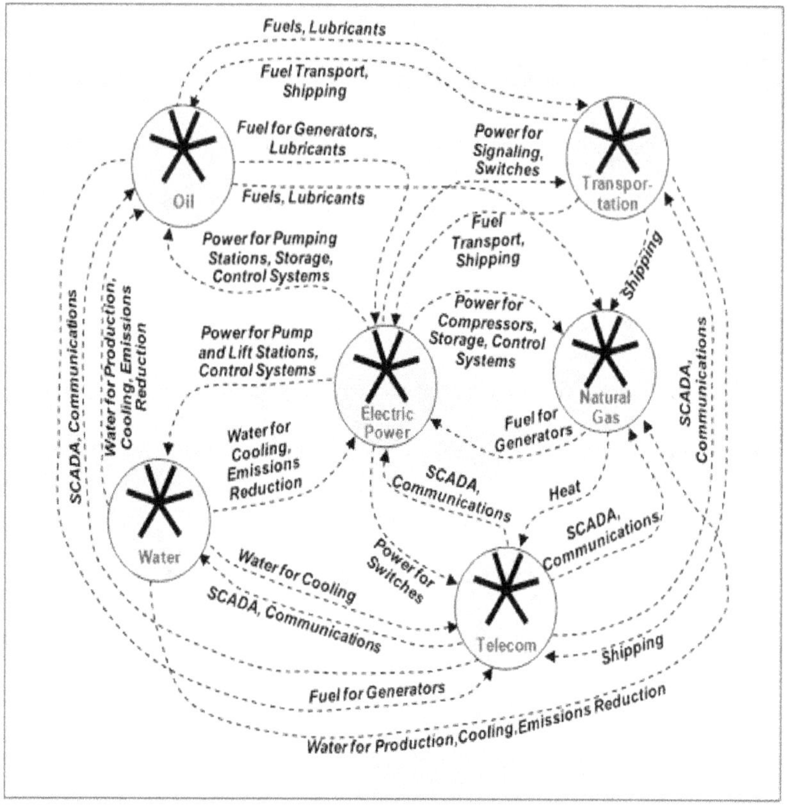

Figure 2. Critical Infrastructure Interdependencies (Peerenboom, Fisher, & Whitfield (2001).

Statement of the Problem

The general problem is that many SMEs are not resilient in their continuity of business during crises related to power outages. Significant crisis events that expose major vulnerabilities to societies and economies include electric power failures (Farrell et al., 2002; Kharchenko& Brezhnev, 2012; Mitroff & Alpaslan, 2003b, Thatcher et al., 2013). Power Outage Mitigation Measures (POMM) can assure continuity of business, but the lack of planning for probable crisis events to include loss of power by businesses hinders resiliency to disasters (Asgary & Mousavi-Jahromi, 2011; Haque et al., 2012; Yoon, Youngs, & Abe, 2012). Power outages have had substantial effects on business in recent decades causing $160 billion in business losses and are estimated to cost the US economy $656 billion by 2020, and $2.3 trillion by 2040 (Richter, 2014). This is significant since coupling power distribution vulnerabilities with increased business infrastructures involving information technology intensifies the risk for short and long-term disruption of businesses (Momani, 2010). In the wake of major crises such as the disruption or destruction of the electrical power infrastructure, SMEs are disproportionately affected by damaged upstream supply chains that can result in losses of income and jobs, among other negative economic implications (Braimah & Amponsah, 2012; Herbane, 2013).

The specific problem the research effort was addressed to is a need for understanding of US small business leaders' perceptions about crisis management planning that includes an electrical electricity grid failure. Despite the size of SMEs, the individual resilience is critical to "broader community and economic resilience" (Herbane, 2013, p. 82). Small businesses represent a key sector of the overall economy comprising 99.7% of all US employers and accounting for 63% of new jobs created between 1993 and mid-2013 (U.S. Small Business

Administration, 2014). Numerous researchers have examined large corporate leaders' perceptions about crisis management, but little research has been conducted on SMEs' crisis perceptions (Asgary& Mousavi-Jahromi, 2011; Bhamra & Dani, 2011; Ingirige, Jones, & Proverbs, 2008; Momani, 2010; National Intelligence Council, 2012). Existing literature relating to the impact of power outage disasters specifically related to small business is limited. Findings from this research effort may contribute to an understanding of opportunities for and hindrances to engaging small businesses in the adoption of crisis management planning strategies, which could positively influence response and recovery efforts in the aftermath of disruption or destruction of the US electricity grid (Asgary& Mousavi-Jahromi, 2011; Ingirige et al., 2008).

Purpose of the Study

The purpose of this quantitative comparative study was to examine and gain insight and understanding into the perceptions of US small business leaders about crisis management planning. The research method and design were appropriate to provide a method for the researcher to identify and assemble the processes and perceptions imbedded in crisis management events and compare variables (Yin, 2011). The comparative design was a particularly useful approach in providing investigation tools such as subject interviews and artifact examination that aided in defining the relationship between the phenomenon and current state (Barratt, Choi, & Li, 2011; Yin, 2011). The participating members of the COO Forum® located throughout the US provided the study data using a cross-sectional questionnaire. Additional data was requested through archival records pertaining to post-crisis after-action reviews and semi-structured interviews to provide varying perceptions for analysis. The findings of this research may provide future researchers additional insight into the perceptions, planning, and experience of key leaders when developing POMM and other disaster mitigation plans. Results may also assist business leaders to identify significant hazards they could face and knowledge of best practices implemented by other leaders.

The broader intent of this study was to inform and help key leaders to identify vulnerabilities within their organizations, and in particular, business operations most susceptible to power outages. Leaders should understand and identify all significant operational systems that are essential to continuity of business and build mitigation plans for when those systems fail to perform. This research can provide guidance to leaders in their decision making processes as they develop business continuity plans.

Theoretical Framework

The study was intended to address a significant small business management of crises including an exploration of the processes decision makers use to develop and execute crisis management plans, as well, SME leader's perceptions relating to power outages and crisis events was probed. A review of the literature revealed an unbalanced and incomplete body of knowledge about SME resiliency when faced with the loss of power. Determining the appropriate theoretical framework began during the review of literature and the examination of relevant information.

There is a broad range of theories that apply to the examination of crises and their management. Gonzalez-Herrero and Pratt (1995) identified a crisis planning theory involving the progression of events to include leadership and management development, planning, and post-crisis decisions. This progress flow of identification theorized on first typing the crisis, and then determining potential causes. Hale, Hale, & Dulek (2005) identified crisis management theories where initial planning through crisis discovery is essential since it helps to determine the internal management processes used during a crisis and how managers position their businesses to address crisis events. VanBreda (2001) added to both the planning and management theories by stating that the resilience theory is crucial within a system as an enabler to encounter a crisis, then quickly recover from its effects. Since an eventual crisis is inevitable within a business environment, establishing a solid recovery process hastens the return to normal business operations.

This quantitative comparative study draws from the theoretical foundations of Mitroff and Alpaslan's (2003b) typology of crises (Figure 3). This nomenclature of crisis, which includes the crisis classifications identified by Burnett (1998) and Gundel (2005) is appropriate for this study for two significant reasons. First, it takes into consideration a full range of potential crises (natural and intentional/accidental man-made) and strategies for reducing vulnerabilities. Second, it is based on empirical research focused on businesses and crisis

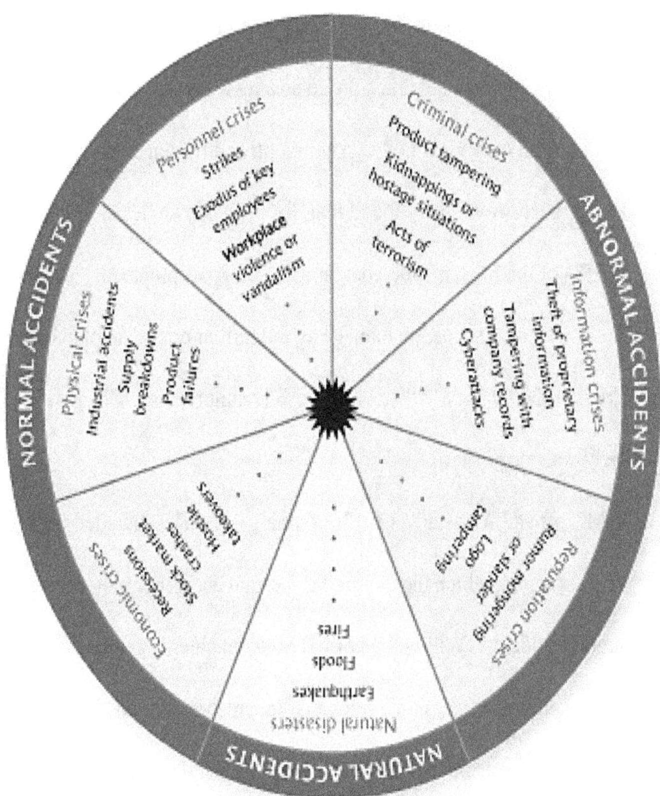

Figure 3. The Wheel of Crises (Mitroff & Alpaslan, 2003b).

management (CM) planning. Drawing from data of a 20-year study of the crisis

readiness of the Fortune 500 companies conducted by the University of Southern

California's Center for Crisis Management, Mitroff and Alpaslan (2003a, 2003b)

identified two groups: crisis prepared (or proactive), and crisis prone (or reactive)

companies. "Crisis prone businesses prepare to handle only the types of

calamities they've already suffered, and not even all of those" (2003b, p. 6). On

the other hand, "crisis-prepared companies develop plans to handle a larger

number and wider variety of emergencies than they have faced in the past"

(2003b, p. 6).

Mitroff and Alpaslan (2003a) concluded that the critical difference between crisis-prepared and crisis-prone businesses is that "crisis prepared organizations not only view CM as a competitive advantage, but practice it as such" (p. 29). However, they found that, for most of two decades, between 5%and 25% of the Fortune 500 companies were crisis prepared. "At best, 75% of companies are not equipped to manage an unfamiliar crisis," explained Mitroff and Alpaslan (2003b, p. 6). "At worst, 95% are unprepared, which, of course, is extremely worrying" (p. 6).

Mitroff and Alpaslan's (2013b) typology of crises included three major categories of crises, which they termed as normal accidents, abnormal accidents, and natural accidents. Within the normal accident category were three types of crises: (a) economic (recessions, stock market crashes, and hostile takeovers), (b) physical (industrial accidents, supply breakdowns, and product failures), and (c) personnel (strikes, exodus of key employees, and workplace violence or vandalism). Herbane (2013) added examples of physical crises in his questionnaire instrument to include failures or loss of utilities (gas, electricity, water, and telecommunications). For the purpose of the present study, the example of a power-grid failure was added to the physical crisis type. The abnormal category included three types of crises: (a) criminal (product tampering, kidnappings or hostage situations, and acts of terrorism), (b) information (theft of proprietary information, tampering with company records, and cyber-attacks), and (c) reputation (rumor mongering or slander and logo tampering). For the purpose of this study, the example of a terrorist attack (domestic or foreign) on the electricity grid was added to the criminal crisis type. The third category of natural accidents included events such as earthquakes, floods, and fires. Mitroff and Alpaslan (2013b) recommended that companies include at least one example from each of the seven types of crises (economic, physical, personnel, criminal, information, reputation, and natural disasters) when creating crisis management planning portfolios as a means of beginning "to consider vulnerabilities that might otherwise be beyond their imagination" (p. 10).

Mitroff and Alpaslan's research (2013a, 2013b) was focused on the top 500 corporations worldwide. Herbane (2013) contributed to Mitroff and Alpaslan's research by applying their typology of crises to small- and medium-sized enterprises located in the United Kingdom. Herbane defined small United Kingdom companies as those with fewer than 50 employees, and medium companies as those with 51-250 employees. Results of the present study further contribute to Mitroff and Alpaslan's theoretical framework by applying the typology of crises to small businesses in the US in the context of a disrupted or destroyed electricity grid. For the purpose of the present study, the U.S. Small Business Administration's (2014) definition of a small business was used, to wit: "an independent business having fewer than 500 employees" (p. 1).

Research Questions

Disruption to or destruction of the US electricity grid directly influences society because of "infrastructure failure interdependencies (IFIs)" (Chang et al., 2007, p. 276). These IFIs include cascading disruptions to water, transportation, and other vital systems. Small business crisis management planning in the US is a critical component of national crisis/disaster resiliency (Herbane, 2013), which is often defined in terms of readiness (or preparedness/ planning), response, and recovery efforts. Therefore, three research questions were used to guide this study.

RQ1: To what extent do small business leaders in the US engage in crisis management planning?

Ho1: Small business leaders in the US do not engage in crisis management planning.

Ha1: Small business leaders in the US do engage in crisis management planning.

RQ2: To what extent do small business leaders in the US perceive their businesses are threatened by man-made or natural crises?

Ho2: Small business leaders in the US do not perceive their businesses are threatened by man-made or natural crises.

Ha2: Small business leaders in the US do perceive their businesses are threatened by man-made or natural crises.

RQ3: To what extent do small business leaders in the US believe they are resilient to man-made or natural crises?

Ho3: Small business leaders in the US do not believe they are resilient to man-made or natural crises.

Ha3: Small business leaders in the US believe they are resilient to man-made or natural crises.

Nature of the Study

A self-administered questionnaire was implemented to provide detailed data relating to crisis management planning. As well, following a comparative approach, documents related to the subject of the study were reviewed and content analyzed. A comparative design was appropriate in determining the "how" and "why" of the phenomenon under study (Yin, 2011). Additional data requested through archival records pertaining to post-crisis after- action reviews provided varying perceptions for analysis. Data obtained provided insight into the crisis planner's questionnaire responses (Poncheri, Lindberg, Thompson, & Surface, 2008). Using multiple sources of data can strengthen the study results through triangulation, which can enhance credibility and confirmability of the study (Baxter &Jack, 2008; Yin, 2011). While historical artifacts could provide a deeper understanding into the perceptions of the participants, the questionnaire provided a detailed representation of the phenomenon of the crisis planning process and was important to achieve the purpose of the study (Baxter & Jack, 2008; Yin, 2011).

Significance of the Study

The current literature on large business crisis management provides results of examinations of the processes used to prepare and recover from disasters to include those pertinent to a loss of power. The present research provides additional knowledge relating to strategies and processes small businesses use prior to and after power related crises interrupt daily business activities. Analyzing the current methods small businesses use to mitigate hazards can identify potential issues in crisis management plans and improve recovery efforts after a disaster. The long-term goal of this research is to help small business communities to identify particular characteristics and processes that create resiliency within a business that have the potential to encounter disasters.

Definition of Key Terms

Several key terms used throughout this study may have more than one meaning; thus, definitions specific to the context of the research are provided below to ensure their context is clear. Definitions are provided from the relevant literature.

Cascading blackout. The failure of one component within the electrical grid that leads to subsequent failures within interconnected components. Between the years 2003-2012, 679 power outages occurred nationally effecting millions of people (Table 1).

COO Forum®. A professional development organization for Chief Operating Officers and executives who collaborate to provide ongoing education and leadership to executives (U.S. Energy Information Administration, 2013). **Crisis.** In this study, crisis is generally defined in terms of "a surprise event that threatens high-level goals and provides little time for [organizational] managers to respond" (Herbane, 2013, p. 83). Crises are further defined for this study in terms of Mitroff and Alpaslan's (2003b) seven categories of physical crises, personnel crises, external criminal crises, information crises, natural disasters, economic crises, and reputational crises. All crises "present a severe threat to the survival of organizations" (Herbane, 2013, p. 83).

Table 1

Cascading power outages 1992-2012

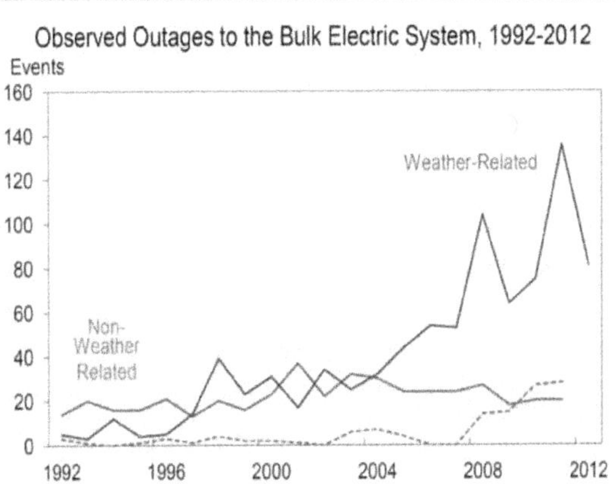

Crisis resiliency. Crisis resiliency refers to readiness (or preparedness/planning), response, and recovery efforts (Herbane, 2013).

Critical infrastructure. Any systems or assets that is critical to the continued and uninterrupted operations of an organization. Loss or interruption of the critical infrastructure would have a debilitating impact on the organization (Federal Emergency Management Agency, 2015).

Electricity grid. The US electricity grid consists of interconnected transmission and distribution systems that deliver electricity through a large variety of electrical components from the generation points to the end user. The electrical grid is also known as the power grid (Department of Energy, 2014).

Geomagnetic disturbances. A geomagnetic disturbance is a storm within the Earth's magnetosphere that is caused by a solar ejection of a magnetic field that interacts with the Earth's magnetic field (National Aeronautics and Space Administration, 2009).

Infrastructure failure interdependencies. Infrastructure failure interdependencies include cascading disruptions to water, transportation, and other vital systems as result of the disruption or destruction of the electricity grid (Chang et al., 2014).

Perception. Perception is a person's ability to recognize, interpret, and respond to information. Perception is a personal aspect to a person's opinion about the meaning of information based on a number of personal factors to include experiences, beliefs, ideas, creativity, and external influences such as peer pressure (Asgary& Mousavi-Jahromi, 2011; Bhamra& Dani, 2011; Ingirige et al., 2008).

Resiliency (relating to business operations). Business resilience is an organization's ability to overcome and adapt to disruptions in operational activities emanating from events such as crises (Department of Energy, 2013; Energy Information Administration, 2013).

Small business. For the purpose of this study, the U.S. Small Business Administration's (2014) definition of a small business is used, to wit: "an independent business having fewer than 500 employees" (p. 1).

Small- and medium-sized business (SME). Herbane (2013) uses the term SME in the context of the United Kingdom in that small companies are those with fewer than 50 employees, and medium companies are those with 51-250 employees.

Summary

This chapter contained an introduction to the study and background information that led to the research interest including exploration of the vulnerability of the US electricity grid, resiliency of the electricity grid, small businesses and crisis management, and typologies of crisis. Following the introduction, the theoretical study's framework was described: Mitroff and Alpaslan's (2003b) typology of crises. This nomenclature of crisis was defined along with its justification for use within consideration of a full range of potential crises (natural and intentional/accidental man-made) and strategies for reducing vulnerabilities. An overview was provided of the research methods for this cross-sectional questionnaire study and operational definitions were reviewed for the study variables, and measurements of the variables related to the study's research questions, and the questionnaire instrument.

Chapter 2: Literature Review

Introduction

This review of the literature contains the context for the present study, a review of the four areas that are foundational to an understanding of small businesses, and the impact of a crisis involving the failure or destruction of the national electricity grid. The review is divided into five sections. First, literature relevant to the vulnerability of the US electricity grid is presented. Second, an overview of the resiliency of the electricity grid is provided. Third, discussions of small business and crisis management are presented, followed by an overview of two typologies of crises that have informed the theoretical framework for this study. Fourth, a review is conducted of the concepts and theories that were examined for this study. The fifth section is an examination of the gaps within current literature.

Documentation. The strategy used in the literature review was to thoroughly explore relevant information including recent scholarly and peer-reviewed articles. This research encompassed databases accessed online to include ProQuest, EBSCOhost, SAGE journals, and Homeland Security Digital Library. To generate potential literature, select terminology was used in different combinations during online database searches to include crisis management, resiliency, critical infrastructure, power outage, taxonomy, small business, and business disasters. Standard search filters of full-text, peer-reviewed, scholarly journal, and recent date range were used during online database queries to narrow the literature results.

Rationale. Small businesses play a major role in the US economic, development and employment growth (Edmiston, 2007; Haltiwanger, Jarmin, & Miranda, 2013). The loss of businesses as a result of a crisis effect the welfare of communities by reducing opportunities for employment, needed goods, and services, and overall communal recovery support systems (Lazzaroni & van Bergeijk, 2014; Lee, Vargo, & Seville, 2013). The focal point of the review was not upon the economic development and growth of small businesses; however, data is included to demonstrate how it influences crisis management (Asgary& Mousavi-Jahromi, 2011; Bhamra& Dani, 2011; Ingirige et al., 2008; Momani, 2010). Business survival and failure are somewhat bound together, though at opposite ends of a continuum. The post-crisis outcome depends on small business resilience when faced with natural or human related vulnerabilities.

The Federal Emergency Management Agency (2015) stated that in the future small businesses could face an increasing number of crises equal to or greater than in recent years. So that small businesses can avoid vulnerabilities related to crises and failure of the US electricity grid, it is important to examine and gain insight and understanding into the perceptions of US small business leaders about crisis management planning. Therefore, this research was an effort to inform and assist leaders to identify vulnerabilities within their organizations and business operations most susceptible to power outages.

US Electricity Grid Vulnerability

The electricity grid is a critical component of society that helps maintain the social and economic climates in electrically reliant communities by supplying uninterrupted electrical energy to satisfy end-user demand. The major

components of the electricity grid include equipment that generates, transmits,

and distributes electricity (Figure 4). The generating systems produce electricity

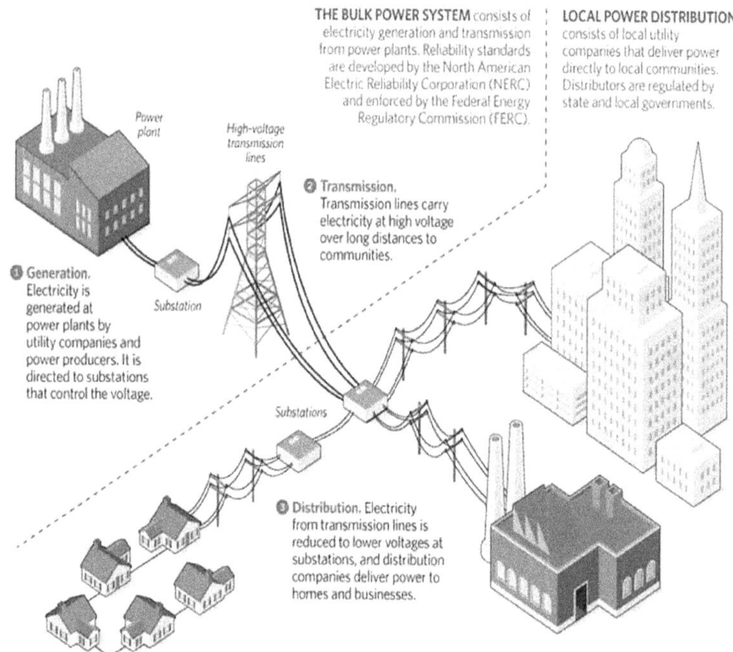

Figure 4. Electrical Distribution System (Lesser, 2014).

that is relayed over the transmission systems to the distribution systems that move

electricity to users. The combination of the generating and transmission systems

make up the bulk power system. Disruption in any of the systems that supply

electricity can cause serious issues to modern life and prolong or hamper recovery

efforts during disasters. Because the electricity grid is a critical infrastructure

essential to the continuity of life, it must be capable of maintaining a level of

resiliency to risks associated with natural and human-caused disruptions

(Department of Energy, 2013; Energy Information Administration, 2013). The risks associated with, and vulnerability of the electricity grid threatens national

safety and security as well as socioeconomic stability (Farrell et al., 2002;

Kharchenko& Brezhnev, 2012).

The protection protocols (Figure 5) of the power systems provide layers of

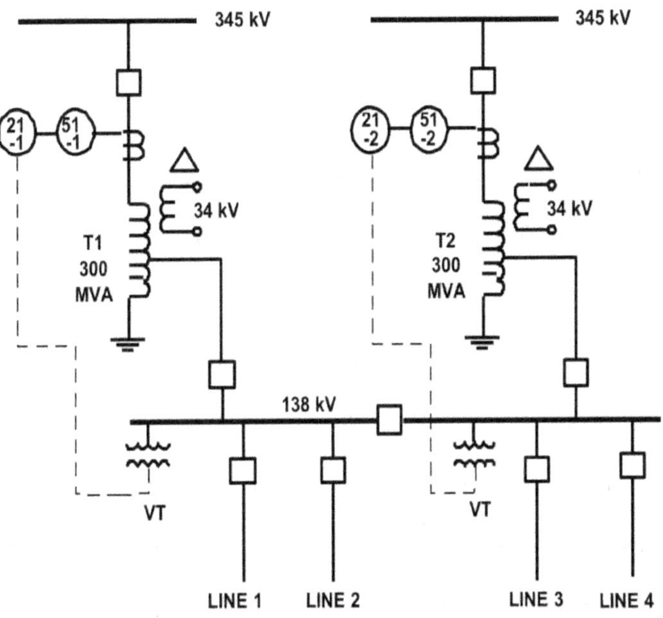

Figure 5. Protection protocol one-line used in transformers (North American
Energy Reliability Council, 2013).

safekeeping to decrease grid vulnerability. Identifying areas of vulnerability are

important to establishing and maintaining protective measures and the

vulnerability of the US electricity grid has been well documented in studies

conducted by or for federal agencies in the past decade (Gaffney, 2014). Several

important studies include those conducted by (a) the Commission to Assess the

Threat to the US from Electromagnetic Pulse Attack (Foster et al., 2004, 2008),

(b) the National Research Council of the National Academies (2008), (c) the

Congressional Commission on the Strategic Posture of the United States (Perry et al., 2009), (d) Oak Ridge National Laboratory (Radasky & Savage, 2010), (e) the North American Electric Reliability Corporation and the U.S. Department of Energy (2008), (f) the U.S. Department of Energy (2012), (g) U.S. Government Accountability Office (Wilshusen, 2012), and (h) National Research Council of the National Academies (National Research Council of the National Academies, 2012).

The National Research Council of the National Academies (NRCA), studied component vulnerabilities that can result in failure and would be of greatest concern related to power delivery. The NRCNA (2012) reported that power substations, large high-voltage transformers, circuit breakers, power relays, transmission lines, and towers are especially vulnerable to deterioration along with natural and man-made attacks that could result in cascading blackouts. Cascading system failures can be responsible for national power system blackouts and while rare, can be catastrophic (Newman, 2015). Cascading failures refer to a succession of failure events that originate from an initial failure. For example, power relays within protection systems can be the trigger for cascading power outages (Khan, Ali, Ahmad, Ullah, & Rahman, 2012) as relay faults are composed of a large number of OR gates (Figure 6) with each gate representing a point of failure. A fault within the protective system will cause an isolation of components resulting in component inoperability. As the initial fault occurs, it trips subsequent faults that cascade throughout a protective system resulting in power outages as electricity fails to be relayed through the transmission system.

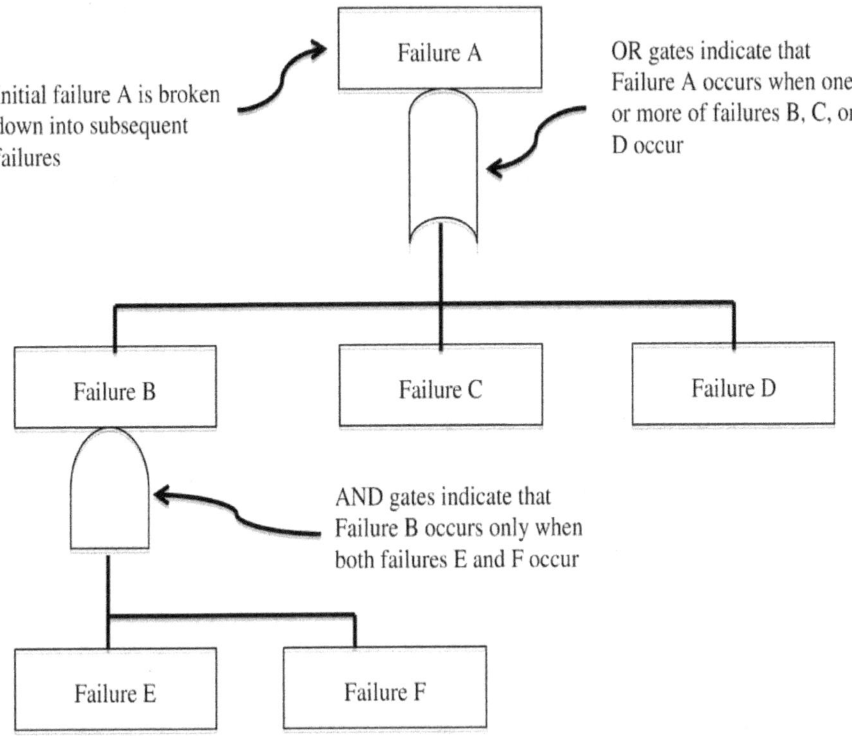

Figure 6. Fault Tree for a single protective system (North American Energy Reliability Council, 2013).

Relays, like other power system components, are vulnerable to the effects of aging, and both man-made and natural events. Cyber related direct attacks on the electricity grid could focus on vulnerable areas that have the greatest influence on electronic control systems such as systems that control relay functions. These electronic control systems rely on "automation, centralized control of equipment, and high-speed communications" (NRCNA, 2012, p. 46). The most critical of these systems are the supervisory control and data acquisition (SCADA) systems, that collect real-time data and send out control signals to equipment. In addition to the SCADA systems, other control systems that are vulnerable to cyber-attacks include substation automation and protection systems, energy management systems, and market systems. Although it is not likely that cyber-attacks will result in extended outages, as is the case with physical vulnerabilities, critical systems can be infiltrated by hackers through Internet connections or directly from remote sites and must be taken seriously because of the potential for cascading outages (NRCNA, 2012).

The NRCNA (2012) recommended that both the power utility industry and federal agencies give "sustained and high-level attention" (NRCNA, 2012, p. 47) to personnel vulnerabilities. The nature of the vulnerabilities is two-fold. First, a wide-range of utility employees and contractors has access to the grid system, including managers, operators, line-crews, and material and service providers. Whether accidental or intentional (as in the case of domestic or foreign terrorists), these personnel could disrupt or damage the power system. The second personnel vulnerability is the result of an aging electricity workforce. "As the current workforce retires," explained the NRCNA, "utilities may have increasing difficulty hiring sufficiently qualified replacement to keep the system operating effectively and reliably and to undertake all the upgrades that are needed" (NRCNA, 2012, p. 47). Critical to reducing the vulnerability of the electricity grid is an understanding of resiliency in the context of power systems.

Electricity Grid Resiliency

A nonprofit regulatory authority, the North American Electric Reliability Corporation (NERC) is responsible for ensuring the reliability of the bulk power system in North America, spanning the continental US, Canada, and the northern portion of Baja California, Mexico. Subject to oversight by the Federal Energy Regulatory Commission (FERC) and governmental authorities in Canada, the "NERC's jurisdiction includes users, owners, and operators of the bulk power system, which serves more than 334 million people" (NERC, 2013, para. 1). One of the NERC's responsibilities is to monitor and report on the resiliency of the electricity grid system under normal and extreme conditions.

In addition to the NERC's efforts, researchers posit various means of ensuring resiliency of the electricity grid. For example, Farrell, Lave, & Granger (2002) explained that power systems should be unbound from centralized control while adopting a quasi-biological model similar to an exoskeleton. In this model, the system initially resists attacks, but can sense and recognize when attacks do occur to facilitate a quick and efficient recovery in the restoration of services. Conversely, Hidayatullah, Stojcevski, and Kalam (2011) argued that within complex systems such as power networks, decentralizing systems and upgrading to smart-grid technologies could address vulnerability and efficiency issues experienced in the current electricity grid. Kharchenko and Brezhnev (2012) suggested that while the decentralization of power systems creates an independent environment that staves off cascading failures, electricity grids should continue to have interconnectivity and implement redundancies that will ensure a stable and ready supply of electricity. The NERC (2013) suggested that centralizing the North American bulk power system might offer benefits and comprehensive oversight of electrical distribution and added to the model of Farrell et al. (2002)

by suggesting systems should adapt their processes based on the lessons learned after encountering attacks. However, while resiliency was a primary topic of research in these studies, resiliency was not related to the need to identify funding sources required to upgrade aging equipment.

A substantial challenge to establishing a resilient power system is how to implement modern upgrade processes within an infrastructure of aging technologies and electricity grid components (Bakken, 2001; Faiers et al., 2007; McKerchar & Evans, 2009). Electricity grid components are essential to the continuity of the energy supply process and many vital components within the US electricity grid are both aging and difficult to replace (U.S. Department of Energy, 2014). The U.S. Department of Energy (2014) reported that the average age of large power transformers (LPTs) within the US is 40 years, which exceeds their estimated 30-35 year life expectancy. An aging power infrastructure is burdensome to the creation of a resilient electricity grid since replacement stockpiles do not exist and some multi-million-dollar vital components such as LPTs require 18 months to manufacture, and are no longer manufactured in the US (U.S. Department of Energy, 2013). The lack of resiliency of the nation's electricity grid should be a concern of small businesses.

In addition to the complications of an aging system, there are abundant threats that test the resiliency of the US electrical grid to include cyber-attacks, terrorism (domestic or foreign), natural disasters such as earthquakes, tsunamis, hurricanes, and geomagnetic disturbances caused by solar storms (Figure 7) also known as high-impact, low-frequency (HILF) events. Power outages caused by these threats effect large areas of society that eventually degrade services and

systems that support the general population. Systems that are impacted from

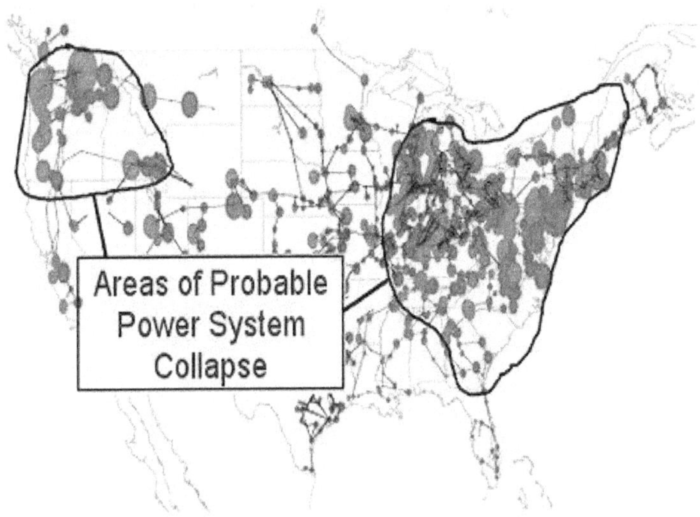

Figure 7. Example power outages due to HILF occurrence (NASA, 2009).

extended outages include industries such as financial, communication, medical,

transportation, food and water, and waste (National Research Council of the

National Academies, 2012). For example, long-term power outages that hinder

the ability to conduct banking transactions can tie up needed cash businesses use

to replenish stock supplies and pay workers. Without electricity to manage

transportation and communication needs, business stock supplies can be delayed

causing considerable financial burden on a business to maintain a working

environment for its employees. Lack refrigeration, food and water, and waste

removal can further threaten the health and safety of society. Medical supplies

can become diminished without resupplies and hamper efforts to treat the sick and

injured (Figure 8). These examples were seen after the wake of Hurricane Katrina across the Gulf Coast cities (Abir, Jan, Jubelt, Merchant, & Lurie, 2013; Quiring,

Schumacher, & Guikema, 2014).

The Internet and advanced technology introduced another risk directly to

businesses and to the electrical networks that support them (Georgescu & Tudor,

2015). Hackers pose a serious threat to the continuity of business and the

reliability of the electrical grid by infiltrating critical systems that maintain

operability. In 2008 and 2011, US electrical and utility grids were hacked by

perpetrators (Thilmany, 2012) and programs were installed on controlling

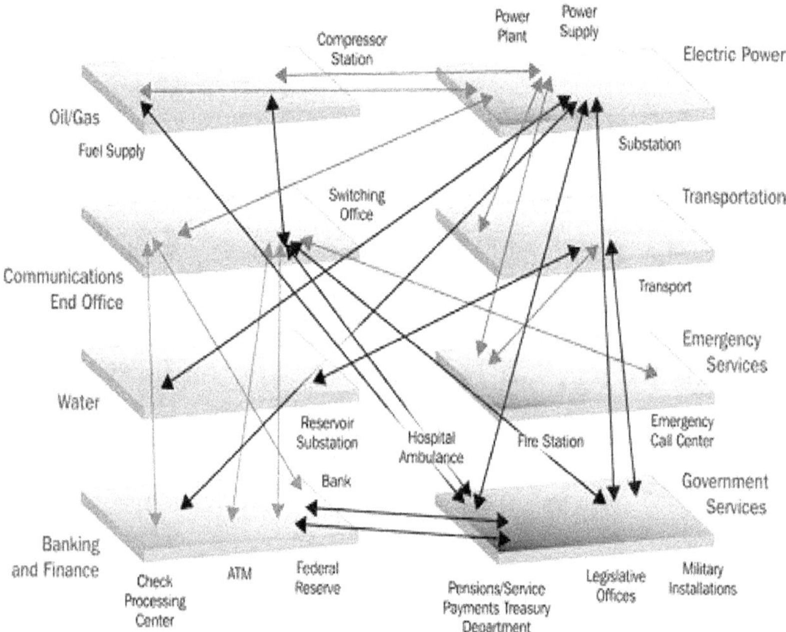

Figure 8. Economic interconnections of critical services (NASA, 2009).

systems. Hackers employed software that would allow them to send messages to

the installed program and make adjustments to the controlled systems as desired.

This included directing shut downs, overloads, and reconfiguring internal controls that could disrupt supplies of electricity for an extensive amount of time. A disruption of power supplies to a region and the businesses embedded within it would be a detriment to the population and cause a significant burden to resiliency.

Terrorism is a significant threat to the electrical grid since due to its unpredictability and long-term damage it can cause. The effects of a targeted terrorist attack could render large regions without power for months (Hancock, 2012). This could cause unrecoverable damage to economies as residences and businesses migrate to areas with greater support services. Terrorist weapons of particular interest are those that emit electromagnetic pulses (EMP) that could result from the detonation of a nuclear weapon. The electrical grid, to include generating equipment such as nuclear power plants, are vulnerable to EMP's, that can overload circuit breakers and unexpectedly shut down cooling systems within reactors. These grid failures could cause nuclear reactors to overheat leading to a meltdown similar to Chernobyl or Fukushima (Slade, 2013).

Tornadoes, hurricanes, and earthquakes can also have a significant effect on electrical grid services. Disasters surrounding natural or weather related events can severely damage electrical grids leaving large areas without the necessary power to provide ongoing services and support. While the 2007 tornado that leveled the town of Greensburg, Kansas left residents without homes, businesses, and supporting services, annual tornadic activity regularly disrupts power services in states between Oklahoma and Illinois (Tanamachi, Heinselman, & Wicker, 2015). Hurricane Katrina was one of the most recently documented natural disasters. It deprived over 2 million people and thousands of businesses of power and services (Abir et al., 2013; Quiring, Schumacher, & Guikema, 2014).

Geomagnetic disturbances caused by solar storms or high-impact, low-frequency (HILF) events pose the largest power interruptions throughout history (NERC, 2012; Slade, 2013; Tretkoff, 2010). As part of its normal process, the sun builds up localized gas bubbles that can result in the explosive release of magnetic fields. The explosions may also release solar flares or prominence eruptions that may or may not include coronal mass ejections (CME). When CME's strike the Earth's atmosphere, geomagnetic storms and HILF's can occur. The charged ions within the storm can interfere with electrical circuits and overload their capacity. Damage to the electrical grid occurs when the Earth is in the path of an ejection that generates geomagnetic storms that subsequently damager electrical components within generating, transmission, and distribution systems, which are also incapacitated by overloads.

The sun experiences over 1,000 CME's per year, or roughly three per day with some more powerful than others (National Aeronautics and Space Administration, n.d.; Slade, 2013). In the years of 1859, 1921 1989, and twice in 2003, Earth experienced the impacts of HILF's when electrical grids and communications services were damaged (Mansilla, 2014; Slade, 2013; Tretkoff, 2010). Both South Africa and Quebec, Canada experienced a loss of power in 2003 as transformers were overloaded due to geomagnetic storms, which left millions of people without power (Slade, 2013).

These threats can be a serious detriment to economic and societal welfare. Societies rely on an uninterrupted supply of power to maintain services that support commerce and daily activities. Businesses are at the center of support for their dependent populations and should have adequate planning for unanticipated and unannounced interruptions or loss of electrical power. Small businesses, in particular, should ensure they are adequately prepared to manage crises as they occur and have sound continuity of business plans in place to manage resiliency during difficult times. There is strong evidence that intermittent power outages are inevitable and therefore should be expected. Design and implementation of a solid program to protect and replace electrical supply components within a short period of time in anticipation of short and long-term or cascading outages should be part of every small business continuity plan.

Small Businesses and Crisis Management

Small businesses are vital to the US economy. They represent 99.7%of the nation's employers (U.S. Small Business Administration, 2014). They are the largest contributors to new job creation, even during economic downturns. The U.S. Small Business Administration reported that between 1993 and mid-2013, small businesses accounted for 63% of the net new jobs added to the US economy, representing 14.3 million of the 22.9 million net new jobs. The socio-economic benefit of US small businesses (U.S. Small Business Administration, 2011, 2014; Van Praag & Versloot, 2007) is well documented in the literature, but the paucity of research on small businesses and crisis management is concerning (Herbane, 2010, 2013; Sullivan-Taylor & Branicki, 2011).

The literature about crisis management among small businesses relating to power outage is sparse (Herbane, 2010, 2013; Runyan, 2006; Sullivan-Taylor &Branicki, 2011). Specifically, little research exists within published articles on the topics of "crisis management," "business continuity management," and "disaster recovery." Of the few studies relating small businesses with crisis management, Ingirige, Jones, and Proverbs's (2008) reviewed SMEs resilience and adaptive capacities to manage extreme weather events. The analysis revealed that SMEs are the least prepared in the business sector. This gap in the literature is significant when considering that small businesses suffer the most in times of extreme crises (Ingirige et al., 2008) because, compared to large organizations, SMEs are more sensitive to "financial fluctuations," "legislation and employment law," "supply network relationships," "technology changes," "changing customer requirements and demands," and "collapsing national financial systems" (Bhamra& Dani, 2011, p. 5373).

Crisis management within small businesses challenges organizational leaders to put in motion efforts to identify and assess hazards that could impede or halt critical operational functions, address crisis as they occur, and recover from crises after they occur (Huzey, Betts, & Vicari, 2014; Runyan, 2006). The processes for a crisis include pre-, during, and post activities (Huzey, Betts, & Vicari, 2014). Crises are those events that have an extremely adverse influence on continuity of business. The pre-crisis events include planning and implementing efforts to mitigate against business hazards. The execution of the crisis management plan happens during and after a crisis event strikes. A significant factor small business must address are the actions necessary should all mitigation efforts fail and the negative impact a disaster would have on business operations is assessed.

Continuity planning attempts to reduce interferences of daily business activities by natural and man-made hazards. Disruptions in business activities have swelled in the last decade as businesses become more reliant on advanced technology infrastructures (Momani, 2010). Reliance on technology can lead to serious interruptions in business operations as seen in recent major power outages. In the last few decades the US and Canada experienced a significant number of power outages that had serious economic implications.

Businesses increasingly use technology such as computers and servers to manage data storage and communications. Advanced systems use technology to include microprocessors that may not be able to withstand fluctuations in power and fail under less than ideal conditions. While technology used in business operations today may be commonplace, the widespread use of such technology was less prevalent 2 decades ago. Reports of power loss have frequently focused on effects related to larger outages when in reality, brief losses of power including minutes or seconds could hinder the continued operation of technologically advanced infrastructures if they fail to mitigate against alterations in supplies of power (Momani, 2010).

The loss of power for a business is considered to be a detrimental source of operational interferences. A large portion of businesses encounter loss of power regularly or perceive that the loss of power interferes with business operations (Momani, 2010). A benchmark report by BC Management (2009) indicated that 87% of international businesses had implemented their crisis management plans in response to loss of power. The loss of power can lead to serious financial concerns as recovery expenses challenge the budgets of small businesses. Based on findings from his qualitative study of 17 small business owners impacted by Hurricane Katrina during 2005, Runyan (2006) referred to the double effect that such power loss crises have on small business owners as both local citizens and business owners.

During and after crises, small business owners and managers are likely to experience greater psychological stress and financial impact than managers of large corporations who "likely do not experience an immediate and indefinite interruption in their income" following a crisis (p. 25). Another example of how small businesses are impacted by crises is the Deepwater Horizon oil spill of 2010, which affected more than 100,000 small businesses in the Gulf of Mexico. British Petroleum expects to pay approximately $7.8 billion in compensation claims to these small businesses, but there is no cap on economic and property damages, which are often difficult to quantify (Goldenberg, 2012).

To address the paucity of research into formal crisis management among small and medium businesses (SMEs), Herbane (2013) extended previous studies of formal crisis management planning activities to investigate the perceptions and experiences of crisis threats among 215 SMEs in the United Kingdom. To examine the SME owner/managers' perceptions of crisis management planning, Herbane (2013) utilized exploratory factor analysis, which yielded six factors that corresponded to small business resilience through "planning financial impact, operational crisis management, the perfect storm, the aftermath of survival and atrophy" (p. 87). Since measures of these factors are included in Herbane's data collection instrument that was used in the present study, operational definitions and measures of internal consistency are included in the following research method section. An overview of two theoretical frameworks undergirding the development of Herbane's (2013) instrument is presented prior to the discussion of research methods.

Typologies of Crisis

Crisis typologies provide a deeper understanding of disaster events and provide a level of predictability as to their occurrence. Some typologies assist to determine future actions while others focus on causality of a crisis (Lerbinger, 2012). Gundel (2005) explained that typologies are necessary for advancing scientific and practical examinations of crises. To enhance practical applications, Gundel argued that a crisis typology ought to be helpful for deducting countermeasures. As such, Gundel developed a four-area crisis matrix (Figure 9) that allowed for the making of "a rough estimate of the exposure of different types of crises, of their frequency and later on of the relevant countermeasures" (Gundel, 2005, p. 110). The four areas of the matrix distinguish four types of crises: conventional crises, unexpected crises, intractable crises, and fundamental crises. Located in the first quadrant of the matrix, conventional crises are predictable and the influences of such are well known. These crises are most often associated with technological systems. Engineering research makes

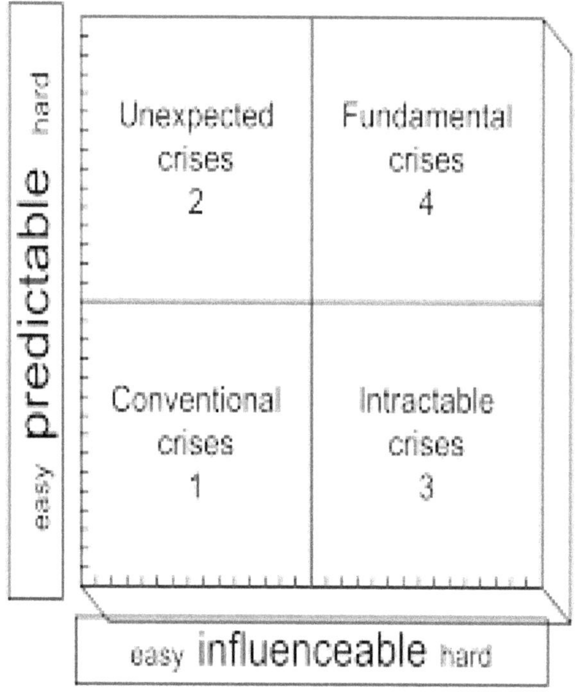

Figure 9. Crisis Matrix (Gundel, 2005).

conventional crises easy to identify, prepare for, and respond to "since the

relevant disasters are known and emerge isolated" (Gundel, 2005, p. 110).

Moreover, "countermeasures are proved and tested and interventions can be

carried out rapidly" (Gundel, 2005, p. 110). Examples of conventional crises

include ferry disasters, airplane crashes, and chemical plant explosions.

Unexpected crises are located in the second quadrant of Gundel's (2005)

matrix. Like conventional crises, unexpected crises are caused by technological

systems, but, unlike conventional crises, their occurrences are rare. The common

link in all unexpected crises is that "the manner of their occurrence was not predictable and therefore prevention has not been carried out" (Gundel, 2005, p. 111). Examples of unexpected crises are unforeseen events that unfold during a forest fire and other fires for which structural fire protection was not considered.

Intractable crises, located in the third quadrant of Gundel's (2005) matrix, are oftentimes more dangerous than unexpected crises. This third crisis type, like conventional and unexpected crises, can be sufficiently anticipated, but unlike the first two types, intractable crises can involve natural and social systems as well as technological systems. Preparing for and responding to intractable crises is difficult because of the attributes of the involved systems and the potential for extreme damage. Examples of this type of crisis are nuclear power plant disasters such as the Chernobyl incident, earthquakes, or crowd stampedes at sporting events. Effective organizational countermeasures for intractable crises include promoting safety cultures within the potentially affected systems.

Lastly, fundamental crises are the most dangerous in that they are "neither predictable nor susceptible to risk" (Gundel, 2005, p.112). This fourth type of crisis, like intractable crises, involves natural, social, and technological disasters. Because of the unknown nature of potential future crisis events that are impossible to predict, countermeasures are difficult to identify. It is here in the fourth quadrant of fundamental crises that Gundel (2005) referred to Mitroff and Alpaslan's (2003b) theoretical framework for exploring appropriate countermeasures.

Concepts and Theories

Several theories and concepts were examined for applicability to crisis management within the present study. The review of available literature started with listing relevant theories to this study. There are ample theories relating to crisis management, but very few address SME crisis situations and in particular the SME leadership's perceptions of their capacity to manage policies that provide adequate response to crisis events. The initial list of applicable theories and concepts included Chaos Theory, Contingency Planning, Continuity Theories, Diffusion of Innovation Theory, Structural-Functional Systems Theory, Theory of Planned Behavior, and Crisis Taxonomies. Theories were assessed against defined criteria and four theoretical models were used to address the determined problem: Mitroff and Alpaslan's (2003b) theoretical framework for crises, Chaos Theory, Continuity Theory, and Theory of Planned Behavior.

Theoretical framework for crises. Mitroff and Alpaslan's (2003b) theoretical framework for crises was chosen as the foundation to build upon within the present study. This taxonomy of crisis, which includes the crisis classifications identified by Burnett (1998) and Gundel (2005), is appropriate for this study since it is both applicable to an array of crises and founded in business related crisis management research. The taxonomy addresses a full range of potential crises (natural and intentional/accidental man-made) and strategies for reducing vulnerabilities. It is also grounded in empirical research with concentrations in businesses and crisis management (CM) planning.

Mitroff and Alpaslan's (2003b) theoretical framework for crises was the groundwork upon which Herbane (2013) developed his self-report instrument for measuring small business owner's/managers' perceptions about crisis management planning. In addition to reflecting Gundel's (2005) and other researchers' crisis types and classifications, Mitroff and Alpaslan's (2003b) theoretical model distinguished between seven crisis types: physical, personnel, external criminal, information, natural, economic, and reputational. These seven crisis types fit within the researchers' three overarching categories of normal accidents (economic crises, physical crises, and personnel crises); abnormal accidents (criminal crises, information crises, and reputation crises); and natural accidents such as earthquakes, floods, and fires.

Mitroff and Alpaslan (2003b) asserted that it is neither necessary nor possible for businesses to plan for every disaster that could result in a negative impact. Instead, Mitroff and Alpaslan (2003b) recommended that business owners and managers focus on including at least one crisis from each of the seven types in their planning efforts to "create a crisis portfolio and begin to consider vulnerabilities that might otherwise be beyond their imagination" (2003b, p. 10). Mitroff and Alpaslan's (2003b) seven types of crises are recognizable in the operational definitions of study variables in the following research method chapter.

Chaos Theory. Chaos theory has found application throughout scientific research including in business crisis management. Chaos theory differs from mainstream classical science like Mitroff and Alpaslan's (2003b) theoretical framework by focusing tenants on unpredictability and irregularity rather than the expected orderly rules found in traditional science (Adams & Stewart, 2014; Gleick, 2008). While lending itself to disorder, chaos theory diligently pursues order in its desire for pattern predictability. The identification of unpredictable historic patters can assist organizations to plan, execute, and recover from crises (Adams & Stewart, 2014; Gleick, 2008).

Chaotic systems are disorderly and nonlinear with variables that do not change in a predicable manner. Chaos by nature does not lend itself to the orderly rules found in traditional stable and linear environments (Gleick, 2008). Random and minor changes within chaotic systems can have tremendous changes with the passage of time. Since disasters can often occur by chance with random patterns, chaos theory is useful in identifying historical patterns, which can determine how businesses could be impacted. As a holistic application, chaos theory envelops a wide range of components outside of the organization to include the community and population within it (Adams & Stewart, 2014; Gleick, 2008).

Unique concepts of Chaos include sensitivity to initial conditions, bifurcations, and strange attractors (Gleick, 2008). Initial conditions indicate the starting environment of chaotic events. Occurrences that cause alterations within the dynamic system are considered bifurcations. Strange attractors originate from outside the chaotic event and provide linear direction to rein in the behaviors of the dynamic system. Additionally, chaos concepts use the irregularity and unpredictability of non-linear dynamic systems to expand organizational effectiveness by presenting unhindered creativity in examining crises from a non-linear viewpoint (Adams & Stewart, 2014). Linear systems may have decision makers that patiently wait for issues to present themselves within an orderly and rule-bound environment. Nonlinear systems require decision makers accept that unbound environments require the acceptance to give up control as chaos presents atypical operations (Adams & Stewart, 2014; Gleick, 2008).

In complex system, the initial conditions within chaotic environments provide the foundation for defining subsequent activities and behaviors, and alterations to these initial conditions can cause dramatic affects to subsequent outcomes (Adams & Stewart, 2014). Chaos theory, therefore, embraces a significant sensitivity to initial conditions and minor changes in the system dynamics. Within the chaos of a disaster the outcome can be unpredictable and the initial conditions or state at which the disaster starts affects the dynamic evolution of the event and subsequent devastation within its environment. While useful in other fields, the chaos theory's broad historic assertion of identifying indeterminate patterns was not desired within the present study, which had a narrow focus on current decision maker perceptions relating to crisis management.

Continuity Theory. Business continuity theorist compliment Mitroff and Alpaslan's (2003b) theoretical framework by contending that businesses are more likely to survive crises through proper planning and awareness of critical business components that are essential to the delivery of core competencies (Epstein & Khan, 2014). The readiness of a business to face a crisis is directly related to and can be evaluated by testing the business continuity plan (Blanke & McGrady, 2012). Blanke and McGrady (2012) provided a Planning Compliance Scorecard help organizations examine organic Business Continuity and Disaster Recovery

Plans (BCDRP). Continuity theories suggest that through the identification of known and unknown potential crisis events, businesses can adequately plan to continue critical operations throughout the crisis event.

The reliance on advanced technologies makes businesses dependent on an uninterrupted supply of power. Ensuring that critical technologies have redundancies in place for eventual power outages is a critical component of a BCDRP. Recent studies in the US and Middle East indicate that loss of power was the leading cause for redundant technology activations as part of the developed BCDRP (Nair, 2014). In addition to technology aspects, continuity theories outline consistent phases of building continuity plans that businesses can implement to ensure company survival. Nicoll and Owens (2013) provided an eight-phase plan that encompassed a multitude of continuity aspects including program management, risk assessment, prevention and mitigation, resource management, plan development, training, exercise and corrective actions, and program revision (Nicoll & Owens, 2013). Other theorists focus continuity aspects to broader concepts like technology, people, and processes as the foundation for solid BCDRP's (Arduini & Morabito, 2010).

Theory of Planned Behavior. Since this study was an effort to determine the perceptions of crisis management decision makers, it was important to understand behaviors associated with crisis planning. As such, the theory of planned behavior (TPB) was examined as a potential foundation for this study. The TBP states that a person's perception of their behavior is predictive of the person's intentions to perform the behavior in the future (Ajzen, 1991). When a crisis planner's attitude regarding a behavior is optimistic and the planner perceives management staff favors the behavior, there is an increased likelihood the planner will have intentions perform the behavior.

Within TPB a person's intentions could be influenced by three characteristics: (a) attitudes, (b) norms, and (c) perceived control. Attitudes about behavior influence how a person perceives their actions have on others around them. These behavioral beliefs make individuals more cognitive of behaviors that are acceptable within their environment (Ajzen, 1991). Subjective norms provide a balance between an individual's beliefs and experiences but can lead to greater influence to social pressures. Intentions can be also influenced by the perceived control on behavior. Individuals may over or underestimate their abilities to have control over their distinct behaviors when compared with environmental behaviors of others (Ajzen, 1991). This perceived control could dictate behavioral outcomes based on group behaviors. A significant weakness of TPB appears when applied outside of the individual and into a group setting similar to this study in its examination of organizations that may have a collaborative effort in building crisis management plans (Huang &Chuang, 2007).

Bridging the Gaps

A review of current literature revealed studies that were examinations of different aspects of crisis management in organizations (Adams& Stewart, 2014), businesses (Gonzalez-Herrero & Pratt, 1995; Grose, 2011; Gundel, 2005) and specific crisis within small business (Herbane, 2010; Huzey, Betts, &Vicari, 2014; Runyan, 2006). There is gap in this empirical literature relating to the perceptions of crisis management planners in small business about electricity grid outages. The current study was an effort to examine and gain insight and understanding into the perceptions of US small business leaders about crisis management planning with particular emphasis on continued operations during a power outage.

This apparent gap in literature implies a failure to understand and gain insight into the planning structure of small businesses that could face detrimental crises rendering the business inoperable. An important gap to bridge is the perceptions small business crisis planners have relating to current critical business operations, perceptions of potential power outages, and the effects power outages might have on critical business operations. Providing this information to the research body of knowledge will better prepare SMEs to implement mitigation strategies that assist in the prevention, management, and recovery surrounding crisis events that impact business operations.

Conclusions

The general problem is that many SMEs are not resilient in their continuity of business during crises related to power outages. The lack of planning for probable crisis events to include loss of power by businesses hinders resiliency to disasters (Asgary& Mousavi-Jahromi, 2011; Haque et al., 2012; Yoon, Youngs, & Abe, 2012). Coupling power distribution vulnerabilities with increased business infrastructures involving information technology intensifies the risk for short and long-term disruption of businesses (Momani, 2010). SMEs are disproportionately affected by damaged upstream supply chains that can result in losses of income and jobs, among other negative economic implications

(Braimah &Amponsah, 2012; Herbane, 2013).

The specific problem is the need to understand US small business leaders'

perceptions about crisis management planning that includes an electrical

electricity grid failure. Individual resilience is critical to "broader community and

economic resilience" (Herbane, 2013, p. 82). While researchers have examined

large corporate leaders' perceptions about crisis management, little research has

been conducted on SMEs' crisis perceptions (Asgary& Mousavi-Jahromi, 2011;

Bhamra& Dani, 2011; Ingirige, Jones, & Proverbs, 2008; Momani, 2010;

National Intelligence Council, 2012). Existing literature relating to the impact of

power outage disasters specifically related to small business is limited. As a

result, the purpose of the present quantitative comparative study was to gain

insight and understanding into the perceptions of US small business leaders about

crisis management planning with which to continue operations during a power

outage. A power outage is detrimental to the continuity of business. Historical

man-made and natural disasters indicate the possibility for future disruptions in

power with devastating consequences to society and the economy. Small

businesses can learn from past occurrences of disasters and integrate the lessons

learned into future planning processes. Small businesses that adequately prepare

for and implement recovery plans after a disaster can position themselves and

their employees to be resilient when faced with insurmountable odds.

Businesses face many challenges in examining the different threats to

uninterrupted supplies of energy. These threats could impede a business' ability to continue operations and support employees or its dependent population. Lasting power outages can be caused by man-made or natural disasters that target critical components that may not have readily available replacement components. Some components are not kept in stock due to their customization and cost therefore making them harder to produce and exacerbate the effects of the disaster. Certain components are controlled electronically and vulnerable to cyber threats where perpetrators could hack into networks and alter or shut down services through a series of remote command instructions. Weather and natural disasters are a substantial threat to reliable supplies of energy as tornadoes, hurricanes and earthquakes can cause extended damage to the electricity grid leaving millions of people and thousands of businesses without power and services. Electromagnetic storms caused by an influx of ions from coronal mass ejections can lead to an overload in electrical component circuitry leading to transformer shutdowns or total destruction of components.

Hurricane Katrina provided strong lessens to the impact a large-scale disaster can have on a region (Abir et al., 2013; Quiring, Schumacher, &Guikema, 2014). Long-term power outages can hinder the ability to conduct normal business operations to include the replenishment of stock supplies and the ability to pay workers. The absence of electricity seriously degrades transportation and communication capabilities hindering stock supplies for many types of industries. Essential services such as refrigeration, food and water, and waste removal may be obstructed causing concerns for the future health and safety of society. Businesses are instrumental in supporting the economic welfare of a society through a number of aspects to include supplying goods, services, and employment. Interruption of business services due to power outages can interferes with quality to life and can also cause serious economic implications if power is not quickly restored (Farrell, Lave, & Granger, 2002; Kharchenko, & Brezhnev, 2012; Mitroff & Alpaslan, 2003b). It is important that small businesses adequately plan for disasters and increase their resiliency to disasters.

Summary

The following chapter contains details of the research method and design, and the population and setting of the study. The instrumentation and operational definitions of variable are summarized. The procedure for data collection and the analysis of resulting data are reviewed. Ethical considerations are cited.

Chapter 3: Research Method

The purpose of this quantitative comparative study was to explore the perceptions of US small business leaders about crisis management planning. The key leaders within a business should be able to identify vulnerabilities within their organizations and in particular their business operations that would be most susceptible to power outages. Leaders should understand and identify all significant operational systems that are essential for continuity of their businesses and build mitigation plans for when those systems fail to perform. SMEs may not be able to maintain continuity of business during crises related to power outages, and a scarcity of empirical research exists about this possible phenomenon.

Significant crisis events that expose major vulnerabilities to societies and economies include electric power failures (Farrell, Lave, & Granger, 2002; Kharchenko & Brezhnev, 2012; Mitroff & Alpaslan, 2003b, Thatcher, Brock, & Pendleton, 2013). In the wake of major crises such as the disruption or destruction of the electrical power infrastructure, SMEs can be disproportionately affected by damaged upstream supply chains that can result in losses of income and jobs, among other negative economic implications, if they are not prepared (Braimah & Amponsah, 2012; Herbane, 2013).

To better understand business resiliency and business crisis planning, business leaders' engaged in crisis planning and execution were selected as an appropriate research subject. Specifically, there is a need to understand US small business leaders' perceptions about crisis management planning and crisis resiliency that includes an electrical grid failure or attack. Despite the size of

SMEs, the individual resilience is critical to "broader community and economic resilience" (Herbane, 2013, p. 82). Existing literature relating to the impact of power outage disasters specifically related to small business is limited.

Small business crisis management planning in the US is a critical component of national crisis/disaster resiliency (Herbane, 2013), which is often defined in terms of readiness (or preparedness/ planning), response, and recovery efforts. Three primary research questions were used to guide the methodology of the study.

RQ1: To what extent do small business leaders in the US engage in crisis management planning?

Ho1: Small business leaders in the US do not engage in crisis management planning.

Ha1: Small business leaders in the US do engage in crisis management planning.

RQ2: To what extent do small business leaders in the US perceive their businesses are threatened by man-made or natural crises?

Ho2: Small business leaders in the US do not perceive their businesses are threatened by man-made or natural crises.

Ha2: Small business leaders in the US do perceive their businesses are threatened by man-made or natural crises.

RQ3: To what extent do small business leaders in the US believe they are resilient to man-made or natural crises?

Ho3: Small business leaders in the US do not believe they are resilient to man-made or natural crises.

Ha3: Small business leaders in the US believe they are resilient to man-made or natural crises.

The findings of this research may provide future researchers additional insight into the perceptions, planning, and experience of key leaders when developing POMM and other disaster mitigation plans. This research may also assist business leaders to identify significant hazards they could face and knowledge of best practices implemented by other leaders that they might emulate. Findings from this research effort may contribute to an understanding of opportunities for and hindrances to engaging small businesses in the adoption of crisis management planning strategies, which could positively influence response and recovery efforts in the aftermath of disruption or destruction of the US electricity grid (Asgary & Mousavi-Jahromi, 2011; Ingirige, Jones, & Proverbs, 2008) and ultimately enable businesses to become more resilient to crises.

Research Method and Design

A quantitative method with a comparative study design was deemed appropriate to provide detailed data relating to small business leaders' perceptions of crisis management planning and resiliency. Data derived from implementation of a quantitative method is deductive, objective, and unbiased numeric (hard) data from participants in response to specific questions followed by analysis of findings using statistical methods (Creswell, 2012; Mujis, 2012; Neuman, 2011). A quantitative method is intended to answer specific questions and measure numerical responses to find relationships among variables and test hypotheses

(Creswell, 2012; Neuman, 2011). In contrast, a qualitative study, a common research method in the social sciences (Gall, Gall, & Borg, 2003; Polit & Beck, 2004), relies on the experience of participants to provide a picture of a phenomenon (Patton, 2002). A qualitative method was deemed inappropriate for the present study because no interviews were envisioned as part of data collection. Quantitative research does not provide for the use of inductive, interpretative Neuman, 2011). Neuman contended that quantitative research is used to test hypothesis, that research concepts are in the form of distinct variables, that theory is causal and deductive, and that data is in the form of numbers collected from precise measurement. Neuman posited that "quantitative research uses a language of variables and relationships among variables" (p. 149).

A quantitative method with a comparative design was used to gather and analyze data from multiple sources and included distribution of a modified version of Herbane's (2013) survey questionnaire as well as archival records pertaining to business plans for crisis management. Data gathered through archival records pertaining to post-crisis after-action reviews provided varying perceptions for analysis. The comparative design refers to the extent to which two or more variables have a linear relationship among participant responses. Variables tested in the study were (a) resilience through planning, (b) financial impact, (c) operational crisis management, (d) the perfect storm, (e) aftermath of survival, and (f) atrophy. They can indicate a predictive relationship that can be used to implement change.

Using a questionnaire and artifact perusal was necessary to achieve validation where multiple sources of data provided the triangulation needed to enhance credibility and confirmability of the study (Baxter & Jack, 2008; Yin, 2011). In this study the researcher explored data from multiple businesses that were gathered through several sources of data. Participants were crisis management decision makers with the authority to develop and implement business continuity plans and were from diverse industries holding no interest in other participant businesses.

Participants

In this study of small business leaders' perceptions of crisis management planning, the target population was members of the COO Forum®. The COO Forum® has more than 13,000 members who are the top operational leaders for their respective companies and can provide insight into operational procedures, including those related to crisis management planning. When selecting the sample for this study the following criteria were considered: (a) experience in years of crisis management, (b) size of company, (c) executive level planning, (d) geographic diversity, and (e) voluntary participation in the study. Of the 13,000 members of the COO Forum® invited to participate in the questionnaire, a response rate of 2% or 260 respondents was expected for validation of the results. All respondents were invited to participate in the artifact document review and questionnaire.

Approval was granted from the COO Forum® to conduct research using voluntary participants from the membership pool through direct contact with participants and through electronic means to include email and online surveys. All participants received documents pertaining to the study to ensure full disclosure of the research purpose. All participants were required to provide signed consent to the study as indicated on a Notice of Informed Consent (Appendix B) that was included on at the beginning of the online survey.

Materials/Instruments

A description of material and instruments used in this study are described in this section and divided into two data collection methods: artifact document review, and a modified Herbane (2003) rating scale instrument.

Artifact document format. Artifact documents were reviewed to collect data for this research (Gay et al., 2009). The artifact documents reviewed of interest in the study included continuity of business plans that related to the mitigation of crises, and in particular, those that addressed power outages. Artifacts were categorized into levels of comprehensiveness considering that the documents were working plans that described and projected the resiliency of each business.

Herbane (2003) rating scale instrument. The Small Business Crisis Management Questionnaire (SBCMQ) was adapted from Herbane's (2013) survey and used in to collect data (Appendix A). Carrying a 5-point Likert scale, the SBCMQ measured participant's level of agreement to the planning for and/or experience of crises within the work environment. The Likert scale used in this study validated identified patterns that were used to develop the research questions drawn from the review of literature. Bryman and Bell (2007) explained that a cross-sectional questionnaire design is an effective method in business research when the goal is to, at a single point in time, "collect a body of quantitative or quantifiable data in connection with two or more variables (usually many more than two), which are then examined to detect patterns of association" (p. 56). Creswell (20012) contended that a questionnaire design is particularly appropriate when aiming to describe the attitudes or perceptions of "a population by studying a sample of that population" (p. 145). A slightly modified version of Herbane's (2013) questionnaire instrument containing a Likert scale, which was designed for examining the perceptions of SMEs in the United Kingdom relative to crisis management planning, was used for the present study. The self-administered questionnaire was deployed using the online program of Qualtrics®. Qualtrics® is a software application that enables users to conduct online data collection and analysis. It is useful for such surveys as market research, customer satisfaction polls, product or concept testing, employee evaluation, and research involving large numbers of participants and online survey questionnaires.

Exploratory factor analysis was used to analyze the collected data. In addition to pre-testing the instrument for clarity, Herbane established the internal consistency, a special measure of reliability, of the crisis planning sub-factors using Cronbach's alpha. The following section is a summary of how the cross-sectional questionnaire design applied to the present study by operationalizing the variables, constructs, and sub-factors, and relating them to the guiding research questions and questionnaire instrument measurements.

Data Collection, Processing, and Analysis

The following procedure was implemented to accomplish the study. Permission to use the database of COO Forum® to contact potential participants was obtained. Northcentral University Institutional Review Board approval for conduct of the study was obtained pursuant to U.S. Federal Government Department of Health and Human Services (2015) regulation 45 CFR § 46.10, which states the probability and magnitude of harm or discomfort anticipated in the research should not be greater in and of themselves than any ordinarily encountered in daily life, or during the performance of routine physical or psychological examinations or tests. A letter of invitation and informed consent form mandated by Northcentral University was emailed to each potential participant (Appendix A) through the auspices of Qualtrics®.

This study was designed with two successive phases: document analysis, and a survey questionnaire. Six sub-factors of the crisis management planning variable are defined in this section (Table 2). A quantitative method with a comparative study design was implemented to gather data from multiple respondents to expose the practices and procedures used by key leaders during crisis decision-making processes. Yin (2011) emphasized that quantitative studies provide a solid foundation for analysis of the research results. The quantitative study is a commonly used strategy for contributions to knowledge in business research as an area of study that can involve complex phenomena (Yin, 2011).

The first phase included the examination of documents to identify historical and existing crisis management and business continuity plans and categorize them into levels of comprehensiveness. Seven levels of comprehensiveness included individual or combination of plans for (a) before, (b) during, (c) after (Figure 10) a crisis.

Levels of Comprehensiveness						
1	2	3	4	5	6	7
B	D	A	BA	BD	DA	BDA

B=Before, D=During, A=After

Figure 10. Crisis/Continuity Plan Comprehensiveness (Yin, 2011).

Categorization of artifacts was significant to understand SME perceptions relating to documented business strategy and the importance of resiliency planning within a SME. The six sub-factors of the crisis management planning variable used in this study were compared to the artifacts to identify patterns and schemes. Herbane (2013) used exploratory factor analysis to identify the factors related to SME perceptions about crisis management planning.

After categorizing the artifacts, a greater understanding of their application and influence on SME perceptions was sought in the second phase of the study, the application of a questionnaire. In this phase the questionnaire items comprising sub-factors were measured using a 5-point Likert scale (see Appendix A, Sections 4-5). Cronbach's alpha, the measure of internal consistency (or reliability), was reported for each sub-factor. In addition, three secondary constructs were defined that the literature indicated are related to SMEs' perceptions about crisis management planning: (a) prior experience of crises, (b) crises threat perceptions, and (c) planning self-efficacy.

Resilience through planning. This first sub-factor of crisis management planning is operationally defined as "the extent to which a formal and predetermined response to a crisis is believed to reduce the organizational costs of recovery and the prevention of crisis reoccurrence rather than simply obviate immediate financial damage arising from the crisis" (Herbane, 2013, p. 88). This sub-factor did not denote the presence of crisis management planning within the organization, rather it referred to the questionnaire respondents' "associations between planning and resilience" (p. 88). This sub-factor was measured using five questionnaire items (see Appendix A, Sections 4-5; #7-F, #7-G, #8-I, #8-J, and #8-K). Cronbach's alpha (α) for this factor is .87 (Table 2). "The closer the alpha is to 1.0," explained George and Mallery (2011), "the greater the internal consistency of items in the instrument being assessed" (p. 223). As such, this factor demonstrated internal consistency, a special measure of reliability.

Financial impact of a crisis. This sub-factor provided a "multifaceted understanding of the implications of a crisis upon an organization beyond the immediacy of lost sales and, notably, the extended time period over which the impact of a crisis might be manifest" (Herbane, 2013, p. 88). Four questionnaire items (see Appendix A, Sections 4-5) contributed to this factor (#7-C, #7-D, #7E, and #8-F). Cronbach's alpha (α) for this factor was .82 (Table 2), indicating a strong internal consistency.

Operational crisis management. This sub-factor referred to business managers' association of crisis management as the "constant vigilance and organization needed to manage known risks as an integral part of running the business (rather than as a separate exercise in strategic crisis management planning)" (Herbane, 2013, p. 88). This factor was comprised of three questionnaire items (see Appendix A, Section 5; #8-C, #8-D, and #8-E). Cronbach's alpha (α) for this factor was .80 (Table 2), indicating a strong internal consistency.

The perfect storm. The perfect storm "represents the dimensions that constitute the characteristic of a high-priority crisis" (Herbane, 2013, p. 88). Two questionnaire items contributed to this sub-factor (see Appendix A, Section 5; #8-A and #8-B). Cronbach's alpha (α) for this factor was .77 (Table 2), indicating a strong internal consistency.

Aftermath of survival. Herbane (2013) described the characteristics of this post-crisis survival construct that indicated the "pressure facing organizations in the aftermath of a crisis in sustaining their pre-crisis operating margins through higher insurance costs and the additional costs that may be necessary to repair and restore the SMEs reputation among its stakeholders" (p. 88). Three questionnaire items contributed to this sub-factor (see Appendix A, Section 4; #7-A, #7-B, and #7H). Cronbach's alpha (α) for this factor was .72 (Table 2), indicating a strong internal consistency.

Atrophy. The sixth sub-factor of crisis management planning "denotes a relationship between a crisis and the partial or complete deterioration of operating resources and the diminution of control over the situation" (Herbane, 2013, p. 88). This sub-factor was measured using two questionnaire items (see Appendix A, Section 5; #8-G and #8-H). Cronbach's alpha (α) for this factor was .75 (Table 2), indicating a strong internal consistency.

Prior experience of crises. To measure this construct, respondents were asked to respond to questionnaire item number four: How frequently has your business encountered the following crises in the last 3 years? Using a five-point Likert-type scale, respondents rated their frequency of experience of seven types of crises: (a) physical, (b) personnel, (c), external criminal, (d) information technology, (e) natural disasters, (f) economic, and (g) reputation (see Appendix A, Section 2). These seven crises were based on Mitroff and Alpaslan's (2003b) typology of crises.

Crises threat perception. To measure this construct, respondents were asked to respond to questionnaire item number five: To what extent do you agree that the following are significant threats to your business? Using a five-point Likert-type scale, respondents rated their beliefs about the threats of seven types of crises: (a) physical, (b) personnel, (c), external criminal, (d) information technology, (e) natural disasters, (f) economic, and (g) reputation (see Appendix A, Section 3). These seven crises were based on Mitroff and Alpaslan's (2003b) typology of crises.

Planning self-efficacy. To measure this construct, respondents were asked to respond to questionnaire item number six: To what extent do you believe

Table 2

Variables/Constructs and Sub-factors, Research Questions, and Measurements

Variable/Construct &Sub-factor	Research Question	Questionnaire Instrument Items
Crisis management planning perception: Resilience through planning (Chronbach's α = .87)	RQ 1	#7-F: Recovery costs #7-G: Cost of changes to prevent reoccurrence #8-I: Planned response is better #8-J: Formal CM* plan isn't needed #8-K: Business more resilient with CM plan
Crisis management planning perception: Financial impact of a crisis (Chronbach's α = .82)	RQ 1	#7-C: Loss of sales to rival #7-D: Legal action #7-E: Negative supplier reaction #8-F: CM only need in event of severe crisis
Crisis management planning perception: Operational crisis management (Chronbach's α = .80)	RQ 1	#8-C: Concerned about predictable risks #8-D: Running business is high-risk activity #8-E: Day-to-day business involves CM
Crisis management planning perception: The perfect storm (Chronbach's α = .77)	RQ 1	#8-A: Concerned about unpredictable risks #8-B: IBHI* threats more important than LI* threats
Crisis management planning perception: Aftermath of survival (Chronbach's α = .72)	RQ 1	#7-A: Direct revenue loss #7-B: Impact on reputation #7-H: Insurance premium increases
Crisis management planning perception: Atrophy (Chronbach's α = .75)	RQ 1	#8-G: Lack of control over event and outcome #8-H: Crisis determined by severity in financial terms
Prior experiences of crises	RQ2	#4: Frequency of experience with crises in last 3 years
Threat perception	RQ2	#5: Perceptions of significant threat to business
Planning self-efficacy	RQ3	#6: Belief about possibility of planning for threats
Planning engagement	RQ3	#3: Plan/no plan

	#3-A: Length of time
	#3-B: Electricity grid inclusion
	#3-C: Frequency of testing
	#3-D: Annual planning budget
	#3-E: Frequency of updating

Note. CM = crisis management; IBHI = infrequent but high-impact; LI = low impact.

it is possible to plan for the following threats? Using a five-point Likert-type scale, respondents rated the extent to which they believed it was possible to plan for Mitroff and Alpaslan's (2003b) seven types of crises: (a) physical, (b) personnel, (c), external criminal, (d) information technology, (e) natural disasters, (f) economic, and (g) reputation (see Appendix A, Section 3). Table 2 relates the variables to the study research questions and the questionnaire instrument items.

Methodological Assumptions, Limitations, Delimitations

Methodological assumptions, limitations, and delimitations are described in this section. Responses, experiences, and perceptions of key decision makers within SME bound this study to a select group of members within the COO Forum®. Voluntary participants within the COO Forum® limited the generalizability of this study. The study required that all participants could respond to requests electronically, further limiting the study to only SME that had email capabilities.

Methodological assumptions were designed into this study. It was unknown if all participants would provide honest answers to the survey or interview questions. It was also unknown if the operational plans of each SME were organic and proprietary or derived from existing external sources. Anonymity was given to each participant and was assumed to encourage trust in the researcher whose intent was to solicit honest and reliable data. It was also assumed that the researcher's membership within the COO Forum® would instill a certain level of confidence in COO Forum® activities.

Due to time constraints and accessibility of data, this study was delimited to participants who had access to email. Participants who did not have email addresses were excluded from the study. As such, this study may not represent all participants within the population in the COO Forum®. Further delimitations included the lack of scholarly literature relating to SME resiliency when faced with loss of electrical power. Additional validation of this work will be required in the future to include subsequent research involving populations outside of the study sample.

Ethical Assurances

To ensure due consideration was given in complying with ethical assurances, formal research must be reviewed and receive approval from the educational institution's institutional review board (Cozby, 2012). No data collection occurred prior to explicit consent by Northcentral University Institutional Review Board. Careful consideration was given to the use of Internet related technologies to include email and the associated risks, benefits, confidentiality, informed consent, and privacy of participants who volunteered to participate in the study.

Approval was granted from the COO Forum® to conduct research using voluntary participants from the membership pool through direct contact with participants and through electronic means to include email and online surveys.

All participants received documents pertaining to the study to ensure full disclosure of the research purpose. All participants were required to provide signed consent to the study as indicated on a Notice of Informed Consent (Appendix B) that was included on at the beginning of the online survey.

Informed consent is an essential part of conducting research on human subjects (Cozby, 2012). In particular, participants must provide consent prior to taking part in the research. An informed consent form was provided to all participants and consent was received from all participants. Additionally, all participants were apprised of any potential harm to human subjects. No participant was under the age of 18 and all research was conducted under the supervision of Northcentral University and met the ethical provisions required by the university. Participants did not receive compensation nor any presumption of compensation for participation in the study. There were no consequences to participants in failing to complete the questionnaire or failing to access artifacts or business meeting notes. Upon completion of the questionnaire, artifact collection, and business meeting notes, participants were thanked for their cooperation and time.

Summary

The purpose of this quantitative comparative study was to examine and gain insight and understanding into the perceptions of US small business leaders about crisis management planning. To better understand business resiliency and business crisis planning, the perceptions of business leader's engaged in crisis planning and execution were probed as an appropriate research subject. A quantitative method with a comparative design was used to provide detailed data relating to small business leader's perceptions of crisis management planning and resiliency. This research was based on three research questions. A questionnaire that provided participants with 48 items to answer was distributed to participant who volunteered to respond. This study was designed with two successive phases: document analysis, and a survey questionnaire. The COO Forum®, provided permission to access its members as a pool of human subjects. The material and instruments used in this quantitative comparative study were divided into two data collection methods: artifact document format, and a Herbane (2003) rating scale instrument.

No research was conducted prior to Northcentral Institutional Review Board approval. Once approval was received from Northcentral University to conduct the study, each potential participant received an email that included a brief description of the study and a hyperlink to take the online questionnaire, which was implemented by Qualtrics®. The questionnaire was self-paced with no time limit. Ethical assurances were observed and the Notice of Informed Consent (Appendix B) was provided to all participants at the beginning of the online questionnaire.

Chapter 4: Findings

The general problem this study was that the extent to which SMEs are resilient in their continuity of business during crises related to power outages was determined to be unknown after a thorough search of the literature. The quantitative comparative study was designed to determine US small business leader's perceptions about crisis management planning and to explore to what extent power outage planning was included in crisis management plans. Their perceptions were tested to gain insight into the importance crisis planners place on power loss and the effects to the continuity of their businesses. This chapter contains the data collected to answer the research questions. The findings are presented through the theoretical framework perspective along with comparison to historic research.

Three overriding research questions and their related hypotheses were tested in this study:

RQ1: To what extent do small business leaders in the US engage in crisis management planning?

Ho1: Small business leaders in the US do not engage in crisis management planning.

Ha1: Small business leaders in the US do engage in crisis management planning.

RQ2: To what extent do small business leaders in the US perceive their businesses are threatened by man-made or natural crises?

Ho2: Small business leaders in the US do not perceive their businesses are threatened by man-made or natural crises.

Ha2: Small business leaders in the US do perceive their businesses are threatened by man-made or natural crises.

RQ3: To what extent do small business leaders in the US believe they are resilient to man-made or natural crises?

Ho3: Small business leaders in the US do not believe they are resilient to man-made or natural crises.

Ha3: Small business leaders in the US believe they are resilient to man-made or natural crises.

A questionnaire was distributed though the auspices of Qualtrics® to 13,000 members of the COO Forum® with a request for return within 30 days. From the responses to the questionnaire 276 were usable producing,18 were incomplete, comprising a 2.1% return rate. Two respondents provided artifacts for examination. The two artifacts examined did not include identifiable information that could be linked to any particular respondent.

Results

Industries in which respondents were engages included 10 categories with higher respondents from consumer services (29.3%) and consumer goods (25.7%). Of the remaining eight categories were telecom (9.4%), financials (9.4%), technology (8%), health care (6.5%), industrials (5.1%), utilities (4.3%), base materials (1.8%), and oil and gas (.4%). Respondents included SMEs that did and did not have existing crisis plans to and included 172 planners and 104 non-planners. Of the 172 SMEs that had existing plans, 46% had plans in place for three or more years, 60% tested and updated their plans at least every year, and 19% of the SME crisis plans cited included mitigation plans for electrical grid failures.

Artifact. The artifact documents reviewed included continuity of business plans that related to the mitigation of crises. To safeguard data integrity and intent, along with answering the research questions, artifact document meanings and their development were derived through the insight of the participants. Artifacts were categorized into levels of comprehensiveness considering that the documents were working plans that described and projected the business resiliency.

The artifacts were examined to identify historical and existing crisis management and business continuity plans and to categorize them into levels of comprehensiveness. Seven levels of comprehensiveness included individual or combination of plans for (a) before, (b) during, (c) after (Figure 10) a crisis. Of the two artifacts provided by respondents, both were categorized as before, where key terms identifying mitigation of crises were used prior to a crisis event. Neither artifact indicated mitigation events for during or after a crisis event. Additionally of significant importance to this study, neither artifact specifically addressed mitigation strategies or potential threats relating to the loss of power. Categorization of artifacts was significant to understand SME perceptions relating to documented business strategy and the importance of resiliency planning within an SME.

Rating scale instrument. The results of the survey questionnaire were analyzed using tools and methodology of similar historical research to include the use of Varimax rotation with principal component analysis (Herbane, 2013). The component analysis was used as a variable reduction method that maximized the data variances. To answer the first research question about how small business leaders in US perceive crisis management planning, an exploratory factor analysis was used on two sets of data to include the impact of crisis and views about risk and crisis management data. There were 8 items used within the impact of crisis analysis and 11 items used within the views about risk and crisis management analysis for a total of 19 items (Table 3).

Varimax rotational exploration using principal component analysis denoted the 19 items could be grouped and displayed in six orthogonal factors using a rotated component matrix. The six factors were (a) resilience through planning, (b) financial impact, (c) operational crisis management, (d) the perfect storm, (e) the aftermath of survival, and (f) atrophy. Of the 19 defined items, resilience through planning included five items, financial impact included four items as shown in Table 3.

Operational crisis management and the aftermath of survival both included three items each, the perfect storm and atrophy both included two items each. The extraction of the six orthogonal factors were placed in a simplified matrix (Table 4) where responses were grouped by factor to reveal the cumulative variance, after which Cronbach's alpha was calculated for each factor to assess internal consistency of the response groupings.

Table 3

Data Items

(a) Impact of Crisis (8 items)	(b) Views about Risk and Crisis Management (11 items)
a. Direct revenue loss	a. I am concerned about risks that cannot be predicted.
b. Impact on reputation	b. Infrequent but high-impact threats are more important than frequent but low-impact threats.
c. Loss of sales to rivals	c. I am concerned about risks that can be predicted.
d. Legal action	d. Running the business is itself a high-risk activity.
e. Negative supplier reaction	e. The day-to-day running of the business involves crisis management.
f. Recovery costs	f. Crisis management is only necessary in the event of a severe crisis.
g. Cost of changes to prevent reoccurrence of the crisis	g. A crisis is a situation in which there is a lack of control over events and the outcome.
h. Insurance premium increases	h. A crisis is a situation that is determined by its severity in financial terms.
	i. A planned response to a crisis is better than an ad hoc response.
	j. A formal crisis management plan isn't needed because I have detailed knowledge of the business.

Resilience through planning. To respond to the first research question, which

was a query about the extent to which small business leaders in the US engage in

crisis management planning, the largest variance of 24.2% between factors

indicates a clear representation that SMEs choose to implement crisis mitigation

strategies through active planning (.86) rather than relying on their ability to be

resilient against disasters (.79). The resiliency and active planning do receive

recognition by crisis management planners as indicated in the importance placed

Table 4

Rotated Component Matrix

	Resilience through panning	Financial impact	Operational Crisis	The perfect storm	The aftermath of Survival	Atrophy
Planned better	0.86					
Resilience via CM	0.79					
CM not needed	-0.64					
Changes	0.69					
Recovery costs	0.52					
Loss of sales		0.74				
Legal action		0.73				
Supplier reaction		0.66				
Severity		0.59				
Predictable			0.67			
Running business			0.63			
Day-to-day			0.6			
High impact				0.76		
Unpredictable				0.72		
Direct revenue					0.78	
Insurance rises					0.63	
Reputation					0.55	
Financial Impact						0.51
Lack of control						0.67
Eigenvalue	**5**	**1.9**	**1.7**	**1.4**	**1.2**	**1.1**
Percentage of variance explained	**24.2**	**9.6**	**9.1**	**8.2**	**7.8**	**5.9**
Cronbach's alpha	**0.84**	**0.81**	**0.79**	**0.76**	**0.7**	**0.71**

on the acknowledgement that crisis management changes (.52) were needed post

crisis. However, unlike earlier studies (Herbane, 2013), SMEs place a higher

value on the costs associated with recovery (.69) over those of organizational

changes within crisis management. The resilience is sharply separated from other

factors such as atrophy factor as crisis managers indicate through substantive

planning, businesses can prevent the corrosion of operational processes and

maintain order and control in light of crisis. The gap between resilience and

aftermath survival is also large as SME crisis managers place greater emphasis on

their mitigation abilities to overcome the potential rise insurance premiums, loss

of revenue, or reputation damage. Thus, hypothesis Ho1, small business leaders in

the US do not engage in crisis management planning is rejected, and Ha1, small business leaders in the US do engage in crisis management planning, is accepted.

Financial impact. The financial impact factor explained 9.6% of the variance as the second strongest emphasis factor. SME crisis managers indicated that loss of sales (.74), legal actions (.73), supplier reaction (.66), and financial severity (.59) have a long-term effect on the recoverability of an organization. As the organization may become inoperable for a period of time after a crisis, contractual dependencies on the organization's products or services may not be realized immediately and could have lasting effects on recovery operations through added time consuming legal burdens. Suppliers of proprietary and other goods may seek to engage competitors to fill their financial gap. Obscured issues may not arise in a timely fashion and their financial impact may initially be so subtle that they are overlooked during recovery processes. Key stakeholders within the financial chain of the business may be affected beyond the initial impact of financial loss as the full ramifications of service interruption emerge.

Operational crisis management. The operational crisis management factor indicates that crisis managers understand that businesses normally face a certain amount of predictable crisis (.67) and that these crises carry a relationship within the daily operational processes (.63). This factor also indicates that planners and managers understand there is an inherent risk in the fundamental process of operating a business (.60). These three items provide an overall 9.1% variance within this factor. This factor indicates that managerial key leaders genuinely understand the need to shield their organizations from a daily barrage of hazards as part of an expected daily routine. Leaders of SMEs recognize there is inherent risk to routine operational processes and mitigation factors must be implemented to protect critical operational functions. While there is a certain level of routine expectations for these foreseeable crises to occur, the daily operational management of risks is differentiated from strategic planning as seen in the first factor. Thus, Ho2, small business leaders in the US do not perceive their businesses are threatened by man-made or natural crises is rejected, and Ha2, small business leaders in the US do perceive their businesses are threatened by man-made or natural crises, is accepted.

The perfect storm. The perfect storm factor provided an 8.2% variance with two item responses of high-impact threats (.76) and unpredictable events (.72). This factor indicates that crisis managers comprehend the importance of escalated crisis that build over a longer period of time and their impact on business operations in light of their unpredictability. The perfect storm scenario starts as a low priority event that may or may not be recognized as a threat, but does not get addresses while growing in intensity without mitigation plans. The perfect storm factor puts crisis managers in a potentially no-win situation due to lack of hazard recognition or understanding and absent plans to mitigate culminating hazards. Thus, Ho3, small business leaders in the US do not believe they are resilient to man-made or natural crises is rejected, and Ha3, small business leaders in the US believe they are resilient to man-made or natural crises, is accepted.

The aftermath of survival. The aftermath of survival provided 7.8% variance and included three responses of direct revenue (.78), an increase in insurance premiums (.63), potential damage to reputation (.55). This factor indicates there is a need for SME crisis managers to address the continuity of business when faced with a crisis impacting financial operations. A decline in revenue with an increase in crisis related expenses requires a solid operational plan to facilitate the return to the pre-crisis status. Within the aftermath of a crisis, managers may be challenged in their ability to operate and provide products and services in a timely manner, while operating under an increased financial burden of higher insurance premiums. Providing stability operations that facilitate this recovery posture will be adventitious to repairing and maintaining the internal and external organizational reputation.

Atrophy. The last factor of atrophy provided the lowest variance of 5.9% and included two response items of lack of control (.51) and determination of financial impact (.67). This factor is an indication of the level at which an organization may not perceive it has control of a crisis situation or the eventual outcome. It is also an indication of how much a manager perceives the severity of the crisis is directly related to the financial impact it has on the business. With the lowest variance, the organizational atrophy post-crisis is an indication managers perceive there is greater reliance on advanced planning and resilience as seen in the resilience through planning factor.

Planning for crises. To answer the second research question pertaining to the extent to which small business leaders in the US perceive their businesses are threatened by man-made or natural crises, and the third research question pertaining to the extent to which small business leaders in the US perceive their businesses are resilient to man-made and natural crises, responses to planning, experience, perceptions were examined between planners and non-planners. The data indicate planners placed greater importance on certain factors in their business operations. The data also support planners who regularly test and update plans place greater importance on loss of sales, recovery costs, legal actions, and supplier reactions over other factors. This shows that SMEs who plan for crisis have a greater awareness of the man-made and natural crisis their companies face. It also indicates crisis managers understand there is a need to address specific threats to harden defenses against crisis making SMEs more resilient in the wake of a crisis.

Managers indicated there was a greater ability to plan for specific crises over others. In particular, physical, IT, and personnel crisis received the highest ranking followed by economic, external, natural, and reputation. Events that occur within the organization received higher ranking of controllability within planning over events that occurred externally. Attacks to SME infrastructures such as crisis effecting physical security, technology or employees were deemed more controllable. Crisis that occurred external to the SME such as natural disasters, terrorism, power outages, and economic recessions were less controllable.

Prior experience and perceived threat of crises. The experience of crisis and the perceptions a particular crisis could occur was examined between planners and non-planners. There was a strong comparative between a crisis manager's experience of a crisis and the perception of certain crisis threats.

Particularly, of interest to this study, there was a stronger emphasis on external (terrorism, grid attacks) between experiences and perception of threat occurrence. Both planners and non-planners indicated a lower experience of external, reputation, and natural crisis threats but indicated a significantly higher perceived threat of external, natural, and IT crisis. The experiences of crisis by SMEs would therefore not have had an impact on the long-term planning of specific potential perceived crisis. The perception of a particular crisis such as a natural or external crisis such as a power outage or terrorist attack could be linked to recent national and international events that could interrupt business services. Media distribution may have an impact on the perceptions of SME crisis managers and heighten awareness of potential threats businesses may encounter. The rankings of perceived threats between planners and non-planners was similar with external and natural ranked highest followed by IT, economic, personnel, physical, and reputation. Similar to historic studies (Herbane, 2013), there was not a statistically significant difference between the experience of planners and non-planners relating to particular threats.

Summary

This chapter contained an explanation to the findings of an analysis of data collected during the research of SMEs perceptions about resilience and experiences during crises. Six crisis factors were examined to included (a) resilience through planning, (b) financial impact, (c) operational crisis management, (d) the perfect storm, (e) the aftermath of survival, and (f) atrophy. Additionally, SME perceptions of planning, crisis threats, and resiliency were examined. An online questionnaire though Qualtrics® was used to solicit responses from volunteers. Respondents included 276 managers with crisis planning authority located throughout the US as part of the COO Forum®. The data analyzed provided insight into planners and non-planners of SME and differences between perceptions of threats and comparatives between planning and crisis experiences.

Of the 276 respondents, 104 did not have crisis plans and 172 had existing crisis plans. Only 19% of the SMEs that responded had specific provisions within their crisis plans to address power outages or attacks on the electrical grid. While most SMEs did not plan for power outages nor did they experience significant losses of power, it was statistically significant that they perceived an external threat to their businesses. This heightened awareness of potential crises without the corresponding development and implementation of mitigation crisis plans requires additional research to understand drivers effecting the decision making process with crisis managers.

Chapter 5: Implications, Recommendations, and Conclusions

The problem examined in this study was the extent to which SME leaders planned to be resilient in their continuity of business during crises related to power outages with specific interest to understand US small business leaders' perceptions about crisis management planning that included an electrical grid failure or attack. Significant crisis events that expose major vulnerabilities to societies and economies include electric power failures (Farrell, Lave, & Granger, 2002; Kharchenko& Brezhnev, 2012; Mitroff & Alpaslan, 2003b; Thatcher, Brock, & Pendleton, 2013). Power outages have had substantial effects on business in recent decades causing $160 billion in business losses and are estimated to cost the US $656 billion by 2020 and $2.3 trillion by 2040 (Richter, 2014). In the wake of major crises such as the disruption or destruction of the electrical power infrastructure, SMEs are disproportionately affected by damaged upstream supply chains that can result in losses of income and jobs, among other negative economic implications (Braimah &Amponsah, 2012; Herbane, 2013).

The purpose of this quantitative comparative study was to examine and gain insight and understanding into the perceptions of US small business leaders about crisis management planning. The comparative design was specifically used to provide a method for the researcher to identify and assemble the processes and perceptions imbedded in crisis management events (Yin, 2011). Responses of key decision makers within SME bound this study to a select group of members within the COO Forum®. The participating members of the COO Forum® were located throughout the US and provided the study data using a cross-sectional questionnaire.

The findings of this research may provide future researchers additional insight into the perceptions, planning, and experience by key leaders when developing disaster mitigation plans. This research may also assist business leaders to identify significant hazards they could face during power outages as well as an understanding of best practices implemented by other leaders. Within this comparative study, a self-administered questionnaire provided detailed data relating to crisis management planning. Comparative studies are appropriate in determining the "how" and "why" of a particular phenomenon (Yin, 2011).

Methodological assumptions were designed into this study. It was unknown if all participants would provide honest answers to the survey questionnaire. It was also unknown if the operational plans of each SME were organic and proprietary or derived from existing external sources. Anonymity was given to each participant and assumed to encourage trust in the researcher whose intent was to solicit honest and reliable data. It was also assumed that the researcher's membership within the COO Forum® would instill a certain level of confidence within COO Forum® members.

Due to time constraints and accessibility of data this study was delimited to participants that had access to email. Participants who did not have email addresses were excluded from the study. As such, this study may not represent all participants within the sample population or the larger population outside of the COO Forum® without email technologies. Further delimitations included the lack of scholarly literature relating to SME resiliency when faced with loss of electrical power. Additional validation of this work will be required in the future to include subsequent research involving population outside of the study sample.

To ensure due consideration is given to complying with ethical assurances, formal research must be reviewed and receive approval from the educational institution's Institutional Review Board (Cozby, 2012). No data collection occurred prior to explicit consent by Northcentral University Institutional Review Board. Careful consideration was given to the use of Internet related technologies to include email and the associated risks, benefits, confidentiality, informed consent, and privacy of participants.

Approval was granted from the COO Forum® to conduct research using voluntary participants from the membership pool through direct contact with participants and through electronic means to include online surveys delivered by email. All participants received documents pertaining to the study to ensure full disclosure of the research purpose. All participants were required to provide signed consent to the study as indicated on a Notice of Informed Consent (Appendix B) that was included at the beginning of the online survey.

Informed consent is an essential part of conducting research on human subjects (Cozby, 2012). In particular, participants must provide consent prior to taking part in the research. Informed consent was provided to all participants and consent was received from all participants. Additionally, all participants were apprised of any potential harm to human subjects. No participant was under the age of 18 and all research was conducted under the supervision of Northcentral University. Participants did not receive compensation or any presumption of compensation for participation in the study. There were no consequences to participants in failing to complete the questionnaire or provide artifacts. This chapter describes the implications resulting from the research findings. In addition, recommendations for the application of findings and recommendations for future research are discussed.

Implications

The implications discussed in this chapter answer the research questions, literature review, and participant responses. Crisis managers rely on a number of factors when addressing planning or methods to use surrounding particular crises. The first research question was as follows:

RQ1: To what extent do small business leaders in the US engage in crisis management planning?

Crisis managers within this study were fully capable of understanding perceived crisis that their SME could encounter. The majority of respondents indicated an understanding that long-term planning was related to resilience; however, the migration of crisis understanding into the planning process or implementation was not universally realized. Although higher functioning strategic planning and day-to-day operational processes were differentiated within the SME planners, more emphasis surrounded predictable events that effect current operations over pre- or post-crisis planning. Crisis planners did not differentiate from non-planners in the ability to specifically plans for a particular crisis. This does not indicate that no planning for a crisis is as effective as planning for a crisis, but rather, this indicates that SME managers rank perceived threats to business continuity similarly regardless of planning.

With the largest variance between factors, SMEs choose to implement crisis mitigation strategies through active planning to build resilience to disasters. The data indicate SME managers place resiliency and active planning only slightly more important that crisis management changes needed post crisis. Coupling this information with the placement of a higher value on the costs associated with recovery over those of organizational changes within crisis management reveals SME managers can stage their companies for high planning and high resilience postures. Resilience and aftermath survival indicated a large gap due to greater emphasis on mitigation abilities to overcome the potential rise insurance premiums, loss of revenue, and reputation damage. Daily operations, however, appear to be even more resilient as crisis managers indicated through substantive planning that businesses can prevent the corrosion of operational processes and maintain order and control in light of a potential crisis.

RQ2: To what extent do small business leaders in the US perceive their businesses are threatened by man-made or natural crises?

Although perceptions of planning may indicate a higher propensity for preplanning at the expense of resiliency, SME crisis managers indicated a strong awareness between a crisis manager's experience of a crisis and the perception of certain crisis threats. While crisis managers did indicate a lower experience with external, reputation, and natural crisis threats, they reported a higher perceived threat of external, natural, and information technology crisis. This was a significant perception of a threat occurrence that included external (e.g. terrorism, grid attacks) on their business interests. Of great interest discovered within this study was the identification of SME crisis manager's increased perception of a threat without practical experience or planning relating to the perceived threat. Neither the experiences nor perceptions of crisis by SMEs would, therefore, have an impact on the long-term planning of specific potential perceived crisis. The increased awareness of a perceived threat could be due to media distribution of a natural or external crisis such as a power outage or terrorist attack. Regardless of their heightened awareness of a particular threat, no additional planning was implemented to mitigate crises. The rankings of perceived threats from SME crisis planners indicated a significant understanding of external and natural threats as the highest followed by IT, economic, personnel, physical, and reputation.

RQ3: To what extent do small business leaders in the US believe they are resilient to man-made or natural crises?

Crisis managers within this study placed significant importance on planning for crisis rather than reacting to crisis. Specific questions were provided to participants to determine their perceptions of resilience factors. Respondents indicated that crisis management plans were needed even in instances where planners had detailed knowledge of the business. Additionally, respondents placed higher importance on response plans over ad hoc responses to crises. Crisis managers recognized the prominent need for both recovery costs and operational changes after a crisis indicating pre-crisis awareness for resilience. The data support SME crisis managers appreciate the long-term need for decisive planning in response to a crisis and that preparation will reduce recovery costs and assist in future occurrences.

Comparison to Theoretical Framework

The study was intended to address small business management of crises including an exploration of the processes decision makers use to develop and execute crisis management plans. As well, SME leader's perceptions relating to power outages and crisis events was probed. A review of the literature revealed an unbalanced and incomplete body of knowledge about SME resiliency when faced with the loss of power. Determining the appropriate theoretical framework began during the review of literature and examination of relevant information.

A broad range of theories apply to the examination of crises and their management exist. Gonzalez-Herrero and Pratt (1995) identified a crisis planning theory involving the progression of events to include leadership and management development, planning, and post-crisis decisions. This progress flow of identification theorized on first typing the crisis, and then determining potential causes. While portions of this crisis planning theory were applicable to this study to include identifying the need for adequate crisis planning and addressing human-provoked attacks on business, the theory did not adequately address leader perceptions of SME crisis situations and in particular their capacity to manage policies that provide adequate response to crisis events. This was similar to the study of Hale, Hale, and Dulek (2005) as they identified a crisis management theory involving the initial planning through crisis discovery as essential since it assists in determining the internal management processes used during a crisis and how managers position their businesses to address crisis events. Results of the study regarding identification of specific decision management processes did not reflect business leader's perceptions as they interpreted the crisis or subsequent action to take when addressing the crisis.

Unlike the first two studies involving planning and management crisis and complimenting this study, VanBreda (2001) identified the resilience theory, stating that the importance of business resilience is crucial within a system as an enabler to encounter a crisis, then quickly recover from its effects. While VanBreda did not seek to understand crisis manager perceptions, the study did complement the findings of the present study by noting that a crisis is inevitable within a business environment; thus, establishing a solid recovery process hastens the return to normal business operations.

This quantitative comparative study also drew from the theoretical foundations of Mitroff and Alpaslan's (2003b) typology of crises (Figure 3). This nomenclature of crisis, which includes the crisis classifications identified by Burnett (1998) and Gundel (2005) was appropriate for this study for two significant reasons. First, a full range of potential crises (natural and intentional/accidental man-made) and strategies for reducing vulnerabilities was taken into consideration. Second, it was based on empirical research focused on businesses and crisis management planning.

Mitroff and Alpaslan's (2013b) typology of crises included three major categories of crises, which they termed as normal accidents, abnormal accidents, and natural accidents. Within the normal accident category were three types of crises: (a) economic (recessions, stock market crashes, and hostile takeovers), (b) physical (industrial accidents, supply breakdowns, and product failures), and (c) personnel (strikes, exodus of key employees, and workplace violence or vandalism). Herbane (2013) added examples of physical crises in his questionnaire instrument to include failures or loss of utilities (gas, electricity, water, and telecommunications). For the purpose of the present study, the example of a power-grid failure was added to the physical crisis type. The abnormal category included three types of crises: (a) criminal (product tampering, kidnappings or hostage situations, and acts of terrorism), (b) information (theft of proprietary information, tampering with company records, and cyber-attacks), and (c) reputation (rumor mongering or slander and logo tampering). For the purpose of this study, the example of a terrorist attack (domestic or foreign) on the electricity grid was added to the criminal crisis type.

The third category of natural accidents included events such as earthquakes, floods, and fires. Mitroff and Alpaslan (2013b) recommended that companies include at least one example from each of the seven types of crises (economic, physical, personnel, criminal, information, reputation, and natural disasters) when creating crisis management planning portfolios as a means of beginning "to consider vulnerabilities that might otherwise be beyond their imagination" (p. 10). Mitroff and Alpaslan's research (2013a, 2013b) was focused on the top 500 corporations worldwide while the present study was focused on 13,000 members of the COO Forum®. Herbane (2013) contributed to Mitroff and Alpaslan's research by applying their typology of crises to small- and medium-sized enterprises located in the United Kingdom. Results of the present study further contributed to Mitroff and Alpaslan's theoretical framework by applying the typology of crises to small businesses in the US in the context of a disrupted or destroyed electricity grid.

Recommendations

Crisis managers of SMEs should examine potential crisis events their company may encounter and ensure continuity of business through planning and resiliency. Sincere assessments of crisis events and exploratory analysis of the comprehensive effects crises have on SME would offer deeper insight, result in superior planning, and greatly improve the resilience and survivability of businesses. Since small businesses represent a significant factor for the overall economy (U.S. Small Business Administration, 2014), future studies should explore hindrances to planning where perceptions of crisis are apparent. While numerous studies have explored larger corporate crisis manager perceptions few research studies exist on SME crisis perceptions (Asgary& Mousavi-Jahromi, 2011; Bhamra& Dani, 2011; Ingirige, Jones, & Proverbs, 2008; Momani, 2010; National Intelligence Council, 2012). Additionally, very few research studies exist relating to the impact of power outage disasters specifically related to small businesses.

Crisis management planners may find this research effort helpful in identifying barriers in the perception to planning cycle and assist small businesses in the adoption of crisis management planning strategies that may positively influence response and recovery efforts in the aftermath of disruption or destruction of the US electricity grid (Asgary& Mousavi-Jahromi, 2011; Ingirige, Jones, & Proverbs, 2008).Power grid failures expose major vulnerabilities to societies and economies (Farrell, Lave, & Granger, 2002; Kharchenko, & Brezhnev, 2012; Mitroff & Alpaslan, 2003b, Thatcher, Brock, & Pendleton, 2013) and with an estimated $160 billion in business losses annually and $2.3 trillion by 2040 (Richter, 2014) the SMEs are staged to incur damaged that can result in losses of income and jobs, among other negative economic implications (Braimah &Amponsah, 2012; Herbane, 2013).

Conclusions

This chapter reviewed the research findings and the implications of US small business leader's perceptions relating to crisis management planning. In addition, recommendations for practical application and proposals for future research were presented. The three research questions concentrated on specific aspects of this study. The research questions directed an investigation of US small business leader's perceptions relating to crisis management planning. In particular, the research questions addressed the examination of US small business leaders' perceptions about crisis management planning that in anticipation of an electrical grid failure or attack.

The research effort was characterized by a concentration on how small businesses address crisis management as influenced by interruption of electrical power. Businesses rely on a stable electrical electricity grid and a brief or extended power outage can challenge the adequacies of crisis management plans. The current literature on large business crisis management examines the processes used to prepare and recover from disasters to include those surrounding the loss of power. This research provided additional knowledge relating to strategies and processes small business can use as part of their crisis management planning. Analyzing the current methods small businesses use to mitigate hazards can identify potential issues in crisis management plans and improve recovery efforts after a disaster. The long-term goal of this research is to help small business communities in identifying particular characteristics and processes that create resiliency within a business that has the potential to encounter disasters.